"This book offers a validating and sympathetic approach to navigating an impactful life experience that is often dismissed. Lenora M. Ziegler offers a comprehensive explanation on why breakups are so challenging—no matter how the breakup comes about—and offers a wide range of coping mechanisms with great efficacy. Truly a much-needed survival guide for clients, clinicians, and anyone who is struggling through a breakup."

—**Yuna Kim, LCSW, PMH-C**, therapist in private practice at www.yunakimcounseling.com

"*The Teen Breakup Survival Guide* by Lenora Ziegler is a must-read for any teen navigating the turbulent waters of heartbreak. With practical advice, insightful tips, and heartfelt encouragement, this book serves as a compassionate companion during challenging times. Ziegler's wisdom and understanding shine through each page, offering solace and empowerment to young readers experiencing the universal roller coaster of emotions post-breakup."

—**Amy Barr, LCSW**, therapy program clinical manager at Brightside Health

"A must-read for teenagers and parents alike! Each chapter empowers the reader with validation, visibility, and confidence as they navigate what they are going through. This book is a profound tool for not only a breakup, but also for life's setbacks, disappointment, and confusion. Through examples, stories, guidance, and tools, this book was written with real-time experiences and wisdom created through patience and acceptance. This book is a gift for this generation."

—**Ilene Mager**, mental health advocate; founder and creator of the #chooseKIND movement; motivational speaker; CN, P; and author of *Kindness Jou*

"What I love about this book is how clear and empowering it is for teens. Most of us will deal with heartbreak at some point. Lenora helps her readers bounce back from a breakup with self-respect, self-compassion, and hope. Her combination of validation and information offers clear steps and accessible tools anyone can use to heal. I plan to use it with my own teen clients."

—**Erica Pass, PsyD**, clinical psychologist and editorial content developer at Answer/*Sex, Etc.*, a nonprofit based at Rutgers University dedicated to comprehensive sex education

"This book is a great resource for any young person learning to cope with the emotional roller coaster involved in relationships and breakups."

—**Amy Morin**, psychotherapist, and author of *13 Things Mentally Strong People Don't Do*

"This is a much-needed, easy-to-understand, relatable, and prescriptive guide to navigating the very real feelings of love. Written for teens but applicable for adults, the author frames cognitive, behavioral, and other tools in innovative ways. Working through the pain of a breakup, you can come out the other side stronger for going through it. This guide offers just the help one needs to do that."

—**Jennifer Hili, LCSW-R**, psychotherapist, and adjunct professor of social work at Fordham University Graduate School of Social Service

the *instant* help
solutions series

Young people today need mental health resources more than ever. That's why New Harbinger created the **Instant Help Solutions Series** especially for teens. Written by leading psychologists, physicians, and professionals, these evidence-based self-help books offer practical tips and strategies for dealing with a variety of mental health issues and life challenges teens face, such as depression, anxiety, bullying, eating disorders, trauma, and self-esteem problems.

Studies have shown that young people who learn healthy coping skills early on are better able to navigate problems later in life. Engaging and easy-to-use, these books provide teens with the tools they need to thrive—at home, at school, and on into adulthood.

This series is part of the **New Harbinger Instant Help Books** imprint, founded by renowned child psychologist Lawrence Shapiro. For a complete list of books in this series, visit newharbinger.com.

THE
TEEN
BREAKUP

SURVIVAL
GUIDE

Skills to Help You Deal with Intense Emotions, Cultivate Self-Love & Come Back with Confidence

LENORA M. ZIEGLER, LCSW

Instant Help Books

An Imprint of New Harbinger Publications, Inc.

Publisher's Note

This publication is designed to provide accurate and authoritative information in regard to the subject matter covered. It is sold with the understanding that the publisher is not engaged in rendering psychological, financial, legal, or other professional services. If expert assistance or counseling is needed, the services of a competent professional should be sought.

INSTANT HELP, the Clock Logo, and NEW HARBINGER are trademarks of New Harbinger Publications, Inc.

New Harbinger Publications is an employee-owned company.

Cover design by Sara Christian

Acquired by Georgia Kolias

Edited by Karen Schader

Library of Congress Cataloging-in-Publication Data on file

Printed in the United States of America

26   25   24

10   9   8   7   6   5   4   3   2   1   First Printing

To my family,

Stuart, Lydia, and Dale: For being my light, my joy, my world

Mom: For showing me how to be strong and kind, hopeful and resilient

Sista Warrior, Michele: For being my pillar of strength, my inspiration

Dad: For encouraging my comeback after my first heartbreak

Nana: For your indelible wisdom that is sprinkled throughout these pages

Desiree: For your unconditional friendship and daily encouragement

To my clients,

Your bravery and triumphs inspire me to keep learning, and for that I'm truly grateful.

Contents

Introduction

Dear Reader,

Trust me, I get it. Reading a book on surviving your breakup is the absolute last thing you want to be doing today. I too wish you were out doing something that brought you joy. The truth is, many teens or young adults will experience a breakup at some point in their lives. Breakups are very common, but that doesn't change how isolating, upsetting, and disorienting the end of a relationship can feel.

Sadly, there is no quick fix or simple equation for getting through a breakup. This isn't a "Do this plus that and you'll feel better" kind of matter. If there were an equation that could help, I would have aced it when I first had my heart torn apart as a teen. I was very good at math in high school, yet it turned out that I wasn't very good at breakups as a teen.

Breakups are hard to do and are painful to live through. Whether you're the person who initiated the breakup or not, or the ending was mutual, this book is for you. There's a lot of pain involved in a breakup, and you deserve support. This book can help.

The Many Emotions of a Breakup

I know this isn't how you expected your relationship would wind up. Everything is changing and nothing feels normal anymore. The uncertainty of what will be and the gut-wrenching reminders that seem to be everywhere are a lot to handle. Add self-doubt and overthinking, and you may feel stuck on questions with no clear answers. Questions like *Will I ever feel like myself again?* or *Will this pain ever go away?* may be on autorepeat in your mind. You may have guilt

(I made so many mistakes) or remorse (Did I do the right thing?) making you wonder if you'll ever be in a healthy relationship.

I've been there. Heartbroken and alone. Overthinking and obsessing. It took me a long time to find my way through my breakup pain and find my steady footing once again. Not until I allowed myself to feel did I start to heal.

I didn't get out of bed for days. My whole body was in a constant state of agony. I had no desire to do anything, let alone something to help myself. I would stare at our pictures, listening to sad songs on repeat. I would cry for hours until my clothes were soaked with tears. Everything I had known had changed. I knew we had issues, but I was unprepared and unwilling to accept that we were no longer a couple. My negative thoughts—How will I go on without him?—haunted me. I blamed myself and I begged for forgiveness. I would stay awake for hours waiting for him to return my phone calls. I spent all my time determined to get us back together. Nothing else mattered.

When my self-loathing and begging didn't work, I moved to anger and resentment. How could he do this to me? I vilified him to anyone that would listen. He broke me into what felt like a million pieces, and I wanted everyone to know. I started to feel better but soon learned that my relief was short-lived. The false well-meaning comfort I received from others ("He did what?" Or "You can do so much better." Or "Now you can focus on school.") helped relieve my breakup emotions in the moment but fell short on helping me learn about myself and how I had related to my ex. Still feeling vulnerable and desperate, I turned to binge-watching reruns (there was no Netflix encouraging me to stay for the new episode in five seconds), eating mostly fast food, and avoiding my friends to get over the pain of losing my ex. I was using quick-fix methods to feel better, and yet I was getting nowhere. My yearning to keep things the same, despite the issues, is what kept me stuck. In effect, I delayed my own healing by ignoring the lessons and opportunities to better understand myself. I saw myself as broken, not my relationship. I let my uncertainty and fear of being alone control me and my actions.

I hope this book will inspire your curious self-discovery and compassionate rebuilding as you cope with your breakup. In my counseling practice I've worked with hundreds of teen clients who are going through a breakup. Despite their varied gender identities, and ethnic and cultural backgrounds, their breakup narratives are often rooted in similar themes of pain, shock, guilt, anger, blame, shame, and hopelessness. I have learned that cultural differences affect the outward expression of pain and loss, yet the internal experience is quite often the same.

Move from Intense Emotions to a Solid Footing

Let's face it, as a teen today, you already have a lot on your plate. Coping with school, friendships, social media, family, and work is enough to keep you busy on any given day. Add a breakup to the mix, and your emotions may feel out of control. There are already enough things you can't control, like the economy, politics, and the weather, to name a few. Your emotions, and how you care for yourself, are things you *can* control, and this book can help. Coping with loss, prioritizing your self-care, clarifying your values, understanding your boundaries, and communicating your needs to others are some of the many helpful topics we will explore in this book.

Remember the earlier math equation (do this plus that and you'll feel better) and how it doesn't work for mending a broken heart? Instead, this book offers a better equation of having time to grieve, plus self-compassion and using helpful coping skills along the way as what truly heals. In math, triangles are one of the strongest geometric shapes and are a symbol of change because weight can be distributed evenly on all three sides. Throughout this book, I'll be using a graphic that I call the Triangle of Change (TOC) to reinforce the learning in each chapter. To use these triangles for practicing the skills you'll be learning, you can download them at http://www.newharbinger.com/53325.

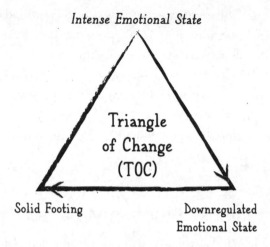

This triangle graphic is used to help you visualize the process of what will happen as you learn and practice the breakup coping skills. You'll feel less pain and steadier, and you'll live happily again. For the breakup emotions you're experiencing right now, think of the downward-pointing arrow as reflecting your being able to move yourself from intense, out-of-control feelings to feeling better and more stable. The bottom part of the triangle represents your more desired solid footing, the calmer emotional state that is your destination as you work through your breakup coping skills and heal.

Try this now: Breathe in, then as you exhale, trace your finger along the lines of the triangle, following the energy flow from the top to the bottom and then across to the left. Perhaps you feel a little calmer as you visualize learning new skills to manage your breakup emotions. If you don't, that's okay. You'll feel calmer and more in control of your emotions as you work through these chapters.

Your Journey Through This Book

Let's talk about how to use this book. It's organized to parallel the three stages of your breakup that I like to call your protest (crying, anger, yearning), your disorganization (negative self-talk, anxiety, depression), and your comeback (acceptance, finding meaning, having a new plan in place). Each chapter represents a different coping skill that can help you transform your feelings of pain and devastation into understanding and acceptance. The nine coping skills explored in this book are intended to be easy to remember and can be practiced every day, even with your other issues unrelated to your breakup. Each of these skills starts from the same place: tuning in and naming what you're feeling in the moment and thinking about how you can respond in a way that is self-compassionate and in your best interests.

I've broken this book into three parts, with each part building upon one another.

- The first section, **Feel**, is to help you calm yourself and reduce your distressing feelings over time through observing and validating what you're going through.

- The second section, **Heal**, will encourage you to connect your thoughts, feelings, and reactions so that you can feel better about yourself and your situation.

- The third section, **Shine**, will empower you to hear your own compassionate voice and create the life you want and deserve.

Now try the breathing exercise again. Breathe in, then as you exhale, trace your finger along the lines of the triangle, following the energy flow from the top to the bottom and then across to the left.

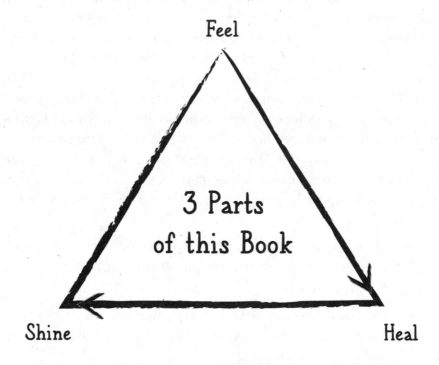

Throughout this book, I'll ask questions to help you reflect deeply so you can better understand yourself in the context of your romantic relationships. Each of the three parts of this book will offer coping skills that solid research has proven to be effective, and guided therapy techniques to empower your learning and growth. Included are vignettes (stories used to teach that don't depict real people), sentence prompts, and practical exercises to help you survive your breakup and thrive in other aspects of your life. Some of the exercises are available for download at http://www.newharbinger.com/53325 or you can write your answers in a journal that will help you reflect on your progress.

I'll be satisfied if this book helps you better understand yourself and how you relate in your romantic relationships. Were there things you overlooked that made you unhappy or that you didn't know how to address? Could you have handled stress or conflict differently? Perhaps a more secure version of yourself may not have stayed so long or tried so hard to fix things? My wish for you is that this book gives you clarity to heal fully and love again courageously. May this book help you heal, feel better, and live life by your design.

Together, we've got this.

With love, respect, and support,

Lenora

Part 1

FEEL

Know Your Breakup Emotions

There is no easy way to say it—going through a breakup really hurts. It can hurt so bad that the idea of feeling better seems nearly impossible. The disappointments and lost hopes weigh heavily on your mind. Breakups can be earth-shattering for both partners, and this book intends to help either teen, whether you were the one who initiated the breakup or not. After all, you were both in the relationship, and at one point it meant everything to each of you. There are many different scenarios that may have led to your breakup:

- Maybe things weren't going well, and you felt you had no other choice than to break things off.

- Your partner may have wanted out, with no more contact.

- One (or both) of you is going to college, and the thought was to break up now before it gets harder to do in the future.

- Perhaps neither one of you was ready for a serious relationship.

- There was a betrayal of trust and here you are, single again.

- Maybe you and your ex have broken up and gotten back together more than once, but this time, it's for good.

Unfortunately, in all these different breakup scenarios, with finality or uncertainty comes a range of emotions and wounds. Whether the breakup was sudden or expected, you feel vulnerable without your primary support person, who is now your ex. Your emotions and thoughts may feel scattered, and it's difficult to put into words how you're feeling. Being able to name what you're feeling and thinking is the first step toward managing your emotions in a healthy way. You can't stop your feelings from happening; what you can do is develop strategies to manage them in ways that are consistent with your values and are self-compassionate.

Breakups Shake Everything Up

Breakups force everything that was once known into total disarray. While you can't stop the breakup shakeup from changing everything, you can learn to manage it more effectively. Imagine you're in a snow globe that has a lovely landscape where you clearly see all the details and pretty colors. Then someone comes by, perhaps unannounced, and vigorously shakes up your snow globe, flipping you upside down and inside out. This is how a breakup can feel. You are left questioning Now what? or How will I carry on without my person? If you initiated the breakup, you may be wondering Should I reach out to check on them? or What if I regret this decision?

And to make things worse, adults may minimize your pain, not viewing your relationship as mature. You may hear "Oh, you can do better! You were both too young to be in a serious relationship." Or "There are plenty of fish in the sea." Even well-meaning people may not know what to say, or they'll say what they think you need to hear to get over your pain. What these people are trying to do is to help. They too may not have expected the breakup and are feeling their own emotions. I assume you appreciate their care and concern, much like I did when I heard the same types of things about my ex. Your loved ones and I—and you too—all want the same thing for you: to feel better.

Right now, your breakup shakeup has flooded you with so many questions and feelings that just getting through the day may be your goal. Wake up, go to school, come home, eat a snack, go back to bed. Or maybe just getting to school is your goal and you'll try again tomorrow, or at least that's what you told your mom. Knowing where to start or what to do to feel better can be super tough, especially since you already have so many other responsibilities—school, homework, friends, chores, work—and completing these is taking you longer than usual. You may be ignoring your friends' texts, and your parents are getting on your nerves. How can you take out the garbage when all you can do is wonder, Will I ever feel normal again?

It's difficult to sort through overwhelming thoughts and feelings, and that's okay. Pause for a moment and acknowledge yourself; by reading this far you've already made a commitment to prioritize your mental health and learn ways to deal healthfully with your situation. As you process what you're going through, your pain will lessen and become more manageable. And by working through this book, you'll better understand yourself and how you interact in relationships.

Be in the Know

Let's first identify what you're feeling these days about your breakup. Some of your feelings may be negative and very intense, like anger, jealousy, and sadness. You may even be experiencing some positive feelings like relief, freedom, and understanding.

By naming your emotions in the moment, you increase your awareness of them, which helps you accept them as is and without judgment. As you pay attention to yourself in this way, you are already slowing down any tendencies you may have to overreact or overthink. This awareness can help you feel happy again and live the healthy and fulfilling life that you're meant to have—and that you deserve!

Read through this list of common feelings, and note the ones you've experienced since your breakup. Write those down in your journal, and add any others not listed here.

abandoned	deprived	helpless	rageful
angry	devastated	hopeless	rejected
anxious	disappointed	insensitive	relieved
bitter	discarded	invisible	replaceable
blamed	embarrassed	jealous	sad
broken	empty	lonely	scared
concerned	guilty	lost	shattered
confused	heartbroken	neglected	shocked
depressed	heartless	obsessive	worthless

Your feelings will likely fluctuate or change from day to day, even hour to hour, as you go through your breakup. Emotions are the real-time data that prepare you to deal with something without having to think about it too much. They'll surface in response to something or someone in your environment, without your choosing to experience them, and they'll spark physical sensations in your body, involve your thoughts, affect your actions, and possibly lead to urges. Because there can be so much going on when you're feeling your emotions, it can be easy to act impulsively instead of paying attention to what your body is telling you. Your mind and body are both giving you important messages; listen to them as they are trying to protect you. Just because you can't choose your feelings (or how you feel about your breakup), doesn't mean you can't manage them effectively. Aha! Knowing your breakup emotions will help you manage them better and in a way that is in your best interests!

Your Mind-Body Connection

Let's break this down so you can have a better understanding of what goes on. Your emotions originate in your brain. You see something or someone in your environment (an *activating event*) that directs your brain to act. Your heartbeat may speed up, your face may feel hot, or you may have muscle tension or a stomachache or sweat a lot (*physical sensations*). You'll likely think negative things about yourself or your situation (*thoughts*) or you may act out on impulse (*urges*). Each emotion is connected to an *action*, and that action is a reaction to what you're feeling. The research assures us that no emotion is bad, and each emotion has a purpose: to give us information so we can make decisions about how to seek safety (Galanti 2020).

Can you think of a time when an emotion helped you? Say you're standing on a sidewalk, and suddenly, a speeding car is coming down the road. You react quickly to move out of the way and to escape danger. Phew! In a sense, your emotions are your own personal alarm system; they warn you of danger or a threat and ignite your action. Our emotions call on us to do something and protect us. Thus, the key to figuring out what to do with your intense breakup emotions is knowing when you're feeling them in the first place—basically listening to your mind and body, your personal alarm system.

The Triangle of Change (TOC) demonstrating the downward flow of intense energy from the top point of the triangle to the more desired solid footing can help you visualize how your mind-body alarm system wants to help. Take the example of seeing your ex in the hallway on your way to your next class. The top of the triangle represents your feelings: I'm so anxious. Downward arrow on right, you notice that you're red in the face, and your heart is racing. You think, This is usually when we see each other. What should I do? You scroll on your phone to avoid eye contact with your ex. Perhaps you notice that your breath is slowing down.

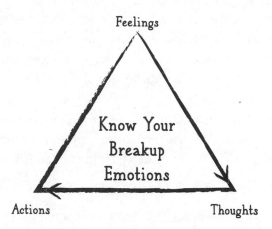

By naming your feelings and thoughts, you were able to act in a way that was in your best interests. Maybe next time, you'll be more ready to be face-to-face and see how it goes. Now look again at the TOC above. Breathe in; then as you exhale, trace your finger from the top to the bottom right of the triangle as you notice the shift in your energy. Then breathe in and exhale again as you follow your energy flow across to the left. Visualize yourself knowing your feelings (I'm anxious) and hearing your thoughts (I can get through this) as you find your steady footing (This doesn't have to ruin my day) with a positive action. Starting to feel better yet? If you are, I'm so glad. If not, that's okay. You will. Let's keep going.

Pay Attention to Your Alarm System

Knowing when your emotional alarm system is being sounded or activated can be tremendous help when you're deciding what to do next. For example, you see your ex's car at your favorite pizzeria as you get to the parking lot (activating event). Almost immediately, your stomach starts to hurt (physical sensation). You're overwhelmed and anxious (feelings). You quickly turn around to leave (urge), thinking that things never work out for you anymore (thought).

When triggered, the brain goes into a state of fight-flight-or-freeze to respond to perceived threats. Your emotions can activate a *flight* response; you leave without thinking ahead about the consequences (your friend shows up as planned and is upset you were not there). You also could have a *fight* response (you demand that your ex leaves; after all, it's your favorite place) or *freeze* response (you can't decide what to do). These responses are involuntary and involve several physiological changes that are important for survival. Knowing how you react to stress can give you helpful information. Ask yourself:

- Since my breakup, have I been caught up in chaos or drama?

- Are my emotions making me feel out of control lately?

- Have I said or done anything that I regret or wish I could take back?

- Am I avoiding certain people or places because of my ex?

- Have I been shutting down lately or not knowing what to do or say?

- Am I saying no to things that I would usually enjoy?

However you answered is okay. There *is* good news. You can learn to control and better manage your out-of-control reactions. When you feel bad, you may react impulsively or without much thought. That overreaction is called *emotional reactivity*, and it happens to everyone. In that moment, you react from a hurt or wounded space, not from a regulated or balanced space. The good news is you can teach your brain to know the difference between feeling out of control and feeling calm and steady. For now, knowing that you can learn to better manage your intense emotions and cope in more healthy ways is a great step toward healing and thriving.

Name It to Tame It

When you can name your emotions as you're experiencing them, essentially you're accepting them as they are, as opposed to fighting against them. Decades of research have found that *Name It to Tame It* is a coping skill that has helpful physiological effects on our brains and our bodies (Siegel and Bryson 2012). The next time you feel anxiety, name it: I'm having anxiety. Then instead of saying to yourself I can't deal with this, try Of course I'm anxious; this is all new to me. How does that feel? A little better, I hope.

In addition to in-the-moment relief, *Name It to Tame It* strengthens your capacity over time to deal with big or intense emotions when they arise. As you continue to practice naming and being able to sit with your intense emotions, you'll gain a new narrative of familiarity and steadiness. The more you practice being aware of your emotions and where you experience them in your body, the more you'll come to understand the nature of your emotions: where they come from, what triggers them, and how they affect you.

As you start to unpack your breakup emotions, let's talk about the feeling of shame. During the early stage of a breakup, shame can sound like this: Will people think differently of me? or I'm so unattractive. That's why this happened. Statements like these may sound like facts, but they are not. They are judgments. Unhelpful judgments like these, when repeated, can make you feel worse, not better. These unhelpful judgments about yourself on repeat can make you believe them as truths (false beliefs) and can affect your feelings and actions. When you accept (name) and just sit with the emotion of shame as being present, you're in fact taming it, by decreasing its effect on you in that moment. You are giving yourself time to slow down and think about things differently. Just because you think something doesn't mean it's true. Unhelpful judgments, once tamed, will sound more self-loving: I'm not feeling great about myself right now, but I'm hopeful that I'll feel better soon.

Let's look at the next TOC to experience the downward flow of energy that can come from naming, not shaming, your breakup emotions. In this chapter, we've established that your intense breakup emotions, if left to fester on their own, will likely make you feel worse about yourself or your breakup. The healthier coping skill alternative—I like to call *Name It, Don't Shame It, To*

Tame It—has a good chance of making you feel better sooner and for a longer amount of time.

Starting at the top, breathe in. Then as you exhale, trace your finger along the right side of the triangle, following the energy flow from the top to the bottom. Breathe in again, then exhale as you trace your finger on the bottom of the triangle across to the left. As you're tracing your finger in this way, imagine yourself being more in control of your thoughts, feeling, and actions. As you move across the bottom of the triangle, imagine your desired calm emotional state, your steady footing.

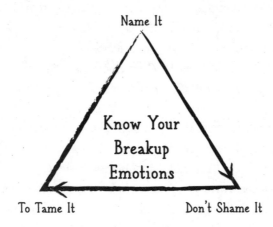

For example, your sister sends you a screenshot of your ex out at a party, which makes you so stressed out. You can't even imagine seeing anyone right now, and you cancel hanging out with your friends. You feel the stress all over your body; you're nauseated, your stomach hurts, and your breathing is getting faster. You change into your pajamas and grab your phone to scroll through his socials. Let's look at three different reactions related to knowing that your ex has moved on. Listen for the effects each has on your emotions: physical sensations, thoughts, feelings, urges, actions.

Reaction #1

Name It: I can't believe he's moving on already. I'm so angry!

You Shame It: You speak to yourself in a judgmental way: I'm such a loser! Your body responds with more tension and stress. You feel even more rejected and disappointed over your breakup.

Hard to Tame It: You feel so out of control that you slam your door and scream, "I hate you!" You are so mad at him and your sister. She shouldn't have shown you the screenshot. This is all her fault.

Reaction #2

Name It: You notice that your breath is getting faster, which is making you feel more anxious. You don't like being alone. I really thought we would be together forever. You take a deep slow breath in.

Less Shame: As you slowly exhale, you think I wish I hadn't yelled like that during our last argument. That made me look like a screaming fool.

Somewhat Easier to Tame It: You check his socials one more time to see who he is with at the party. Not seeing anything posted, you wonder if he blocked you. You ask your sister if she wants to watch a movie with you.

Reaction #3

Name It: You keep naming your emotion, without judging yourself: I'm anxious, I'm anxious, I'm anxious. This is all new for me. It's normal to feel this way. Other people in the same situation would be anxious too. You feel your breathing slowly coming back to normal, and you take a few sips of water.

Don't Shame It: You notice your body slowly calming itself, and you feel less agitated and anxious. You accept these feelings as expected responses to what you're going through. You don't judge yourself for feeling them.

To Tame It: You ask your sister if she wants to watch a movie. She says yes. You make the popcorn; she refills your water bottles. You leave your phone in your room so you can enjoy the movie.

Which of the above scenarios most likely represents how you've been dealing with your breakup? Whichever your answer, go back and reread the third option. I used to love the choose-your-own-ending books as a kid. Can you tell? Anyway, as you read the third option, review the TOC above, or draw the same image in your journal.

Starting at the top, breathe in. Then, as you exhale, trace your finger along the lines of the triangle, following the energy flow from the top to the bottom. Breathe in again, then exhale as you trace your finger on the bottom of the triangle across to the left. Perhaps you feel a little calmer as you visualize learning new skills to manage your breakup emotions. If you don't, that's okay. You'll feel calmer and more in control of your emotions as you continue to work through these chapters.

Access Your Support System

So far, we have been talking about tuning in to and naming your breakup emotions. Naming your emotions by no means is meant to minimize them. The work toward healing begins with you being able to sit with your intense breakup emotions so you can learn to better manage them. Remember, just because you can't choose how you feel about your breakup doesn't mean you can't manage those feelings effectively. Sometimes coping with a breakup can seem too hard to manage on your own, and it's okay to not be okay. If you're struggling or feel alone, you may need additional help beyond this book. This next section will detail important information about accessing your support system at home, school, and in your community.

Your close friends and family may not know exactly what you're going through, but they too have likely experienced some sort of loss or been hurt by another person. It can also be helpful to seek out support from a member of your extended family, like an aunt, uncle, cousin, or grandmother. You can also seek support from other adults you trust, for example, a coach, teacher, guidance counselor, community leader, or someone you know through your religious affiliation or place of worship. The professional helpers in your life, like those people who work at your school, your physician, or your other healthcare providers, can link you to mental health and counseling resources in your community or state, as well as either online or local teen support groups. Please refer to the Resources section in the back of this book for helpful online directories that can help you locate licensed therapists in the state where you live. Licensed therapists are professionals with advanced training in counseling, and they usually have one of the following initials after their name: LCSW, PhD, PsyD, LPC, LCADC, LMFT.

When You Need Extra Support

Getting extra support is important and can be life-saving if you're having a difficult time coping with your breakup. Here are some warning signs that you may need extra help:

- Do you think about hurting yourself in any way?
- Do you ever wish you were dead?
- Do you see no way out of your pain?
- Are you feeling hopeless or helpless?

- Do you drink alcohol or smoke marijuana to numb or escape your feelings?

- Do you take pills that weren't prescribed for you?

- Do you take more than you're supposed to of pills that were prescribed for you by a doctor?

- Have you thought about killing yourself?

If you answered yes to any of these questions, that's a warning sign that you need to talk to someone right away.

> **NOTE:** If you're thinking about hurting yourself, have suicidal thoughts, or wish you were dead, it's important to reach out for support. Call 911, call or text **988** (the 24-hour suicide and crisis lifeline), or go to your local emergency room.

There are benefits to having a support system. Research has shown that when teenagers feel connected to social support, this connection has a positive effect on their *resilience*, the process of adapting to difficult or challenging life experiences (Raja 2021). Identifying who is in your support system can seem difficult when you feel alone. Remember, support can come from anyone you see on a regular basis and who you trust to care for you. The key is accepting that people cannot read your mind. If you need help, it's okay to ask for it—and I strongly encourage you to let one or a few people in your support system know that you need help. If you decide to start or are currently in therapy, you may even want to tell your therapist about this book; the two of you can work on the exercises together in session.

Let's Recap

This first chapter, "Know Your Breakup Emotions," has explored and normalized the full range of usual and expected emotions after a breakup. You have been encouraged to name your breakup emotions and to start listening to your breakup narrative, the things you think or tell yourself about your situation. By naming your breakup emotions, you're learning to connect your feelings to your thoughts and actions so you can make choices that are in your best interests. A breakup narrative can include helpful and unhelpful thoughts about yourself as you continue to struggle with the changes related to your breakup.

You are likely experiencing urges to get your ex back or to check in on them. You may even be overexplaining yourself or overthinking the past or the future without them. As you continue in this book, you'll explore coping skills that can help you slow down and better manage your reactions. You'll be encouraged to show yourself compassion as you begin to process and accept the reality of your loss.

Talk About What You Have Lost

Breakups can be earth-shattering for both partners. It's my hope that from reading this book, you'll start to pivot your view of your breakup to see less pain and more hope. In the previous chapter, you started by naming and normalizing your breakup emotions and how you're feeling. As you acknowledge and name your emotions (I'm anxious and feel so alone), you can notice where you're feeling the emotion in your body (My stomach hurts) and listen for your thoughts (I can't go to school today). The practice of connecting your feelings and thoughts to your behaviors gives you the solid footing to become more grounded in the reality of the loss and its effects on you.

In this chapter you'll explore how you're coping with the loss of your relationship and the changes in your routine. You'll look at the common stages of grief after a breakup, and you'll be encouraged to understand what stage you're in. While the stages of grief don't go in any specific order and don't have a timeline, the goal is being able to process the feelings at every stage as you move your energy toward acceptance and healing. You'll begin to explore how your brain can change and the science behind training your brain to help you resist the urge to contact your ex (as doing this can delay your healing).

The Loss Is Real

The hardest part of dealing with a breakup is coping with the things that have changed because your relationship is over. Letting yourself process and feel what you've lost is an important step toward healing. Do any of the following losses resonate with you?

- Loss of my best friend

- Loss of my identity as someone's significant other

- Loss of my routine

- Loss of my friend group

- Loss of having an intimate partner

- Loss of my support person

- Loss of part of my history

- Loss of my ride to the mall or school

- Loss of someone to hang out with on the weekends

- Loss of my study buddy

If you can think of other losses you're experiencing because of your breakup, write them down in your journal. You may want to write about what you appreciated or enjoyed from being in the relationship (spending time with someone, celebrating holidays or birthdays, receiving emotional support, laughing, feeling close to someone). This list can give you helpful insights about yourself and your values, which are the beliefs that define what is most important to you. Perhaps in your relationships you value love, morals, loyalty, fairness, adventure, honesty, humor, independence, spirituality, and safety, to name a few.

The Stages of Grief After a Breakup

Grieving over the losses and the change to your relationship status is normal. Grief is different for each person and can affect four main areas: your body, your emotions, your thoughts, and how you relate to others. After a breakup, it can be helpful to understand where you are in your grief process. There are five stages of grief after a breakup: denial, anger, bargaining, depression, and acceptance.

Denial: This automatic response to unwanted news is a common way for people to avoid dealing with troubling or intense feelings. Denial isn't always a bad thing. Being in denial can give you a little extra time and space to come to grips with the change in your relationship status, especially if the news of your breakup came as a shock.

Anger: It's normal to feel angry at your ex for what has happened and for all that you're suffering through. It can be helpful to validate that it's okay to feel anger, which is an expected emotion after a breakup.

Bargaining: You might try to convince yourself and/or your ex that things will be better if you're given another chance. You may be reaching out to try to befriend your ex despite knowing that they have specifically asked for a no-contact rule after the breakup.

Depression: Feeling sad and down is normal after a breakup. At this point in your grieving, you realize that your situation isn't going to change. You may be struggling to get back to your normal routine. You're starting to realize that you'll likely benefit from increasing your activity, getting in touch with your support system, and resuming doing things that previously brought you joy or pleasure.

> **NOTE:** If you're experiencing a depressed mood or suicidal thoughts, it's important to reach out for support. Tell a trusted adult or a friend about how you're feeling. Call 911 or the 24-hour suicide and crisis lifeline at **988** so you're not alone, or go to your local emergency room.

Acceptance: The relationships we have with the significant people in our life make us who we are. In the final stage of grief after a breakup, you've started to accept the reality of the loss and acknowledge the part you played in it. This acceptance phase offers you a big opportunity to learn from the mistakes of the past and carry those lessons into your future so you can grow as an individual. The pain of the breakup may not be completely gone yet, but as you continue to nurture yourself with acceptance, your story will have less pain and more self-compassion.

What Stage of Grief Are You In?

Let's look at three vignettes of recent breakups. For each, decide which option most closely resembles how you might respond in that situation, and write down its identifying letter in your journal. You'll code your selected answers at the end of the exercise to give you an idea of what stage of grief you might be gravitating toward at this time.

Story 1: It's been a week since your breakup with Steve, which happened abruptly when he texted you that he wanted to take a break to deal with some personal stuff. Steve asked that you and he not speak for the next two weeks. The two of you met last spring when you joined your high school track team. There's a holiday party this coming weekend for your track team, and you both have a lot of friends on the team. You and Steve haven't spoken since your breakup, so you're not sure whether you should go to the party.

A. You think it's no big deal if you and Steve both go to the party and have a great time together. You may even suggest in front of the team that you and he stand under the mistletoe for a kiss.

B. You can't deal with the fact that Steve broke up with you by text. You decide that you'll show up unannounced at Steve's after-school job at the pizzeria and demand that you and he talk about who gets to go to the track team party.

C. You see the party as a perfect opportunity to wear Steve's favorite black dress and the red lipstick he loves. There'll be no way he can

resist you, especially if you ask him about how his grandmother has been doing since her recent hip surgery.

D. You're feeling so down and hopeless that a holiday party is the last place you can see yourself going to this weekend. Steve can go to the party; he'll probably have a new girlfriend by next week anyway.

E. It seems that Steve is going through something right now. It's hurtful that he broke up with you by text, and you wish that he would have elaborated on what he meant by taking a break. You decide to text Steve to tell him you plan to go to the party to spend time with your friends on the team. You share that you're open to feedback if he will be upset by your attending.

Story 2: You and your girlfriend Jenny go to different high schools, and she has been very busy lately with her school play. You and she have not seen each other in over a week, and she canceled your last two scheduled FaceTime calls. This is bringing up your vulnerabilities of feeling invisible, like when your mom would be late to your band concerts. You recently discovered that Jenny is in many of the same scenes as her ex-girlfriend. Plus, they have been eating dinner together at the sub shop up the road from their school after their rehearsals. What would you do?

A. You think, It's not an issue. I'll get over it.

B. You cannot hold it in any longer. You call Jenny and leave her a voice-mail letting her have it. How can she do this to you?

C. You decide to make plans with other people over the next week so that you're booked up. This way, when Jenny realizes how busy you are, she'll want to see you again.

D. You're feeling sad about the recent distance between you and Jenny. You've been talking to your friend Christy about your feelings, and you're taking her advice to avoid risky behaviors like overeating, drugs, and alcohol.

E.   You plan to talk to Jenny over the next few days about your feelings. You'll consider your own part in the recent distance between you two and offer some ideas of things you two can do together.

Story 3: You've started vaping more regularly, and your boyfriend, Jason, is saying that it's a deal-breaker for him. Early in your relationship, Jason had told you that his father smoked three packs of cigarettes a day and that he died years ago from lung cancer. You've noticed that he becomes anxious and jittery over the mention of tobacco, nicotine, or any type of smoking, even e-cigarettes. Now he says that unless you quit smoking, he'll have to break up with you.

A.   You think, It's not that bad. I don't smoke that much. Jason and I can stay together, and nothing has to change.

B.   You feel so frustrated that Jason is trying to control you and your choices.

C.   You say to yourself, Maybe if I smoke only when I'm not around Jason, we can stay together. He won't be able to smell the vape pen anyway.

D.   You feel down and helpless about the conversation with Jason. You shut down and avoid his phone calls and texts over the next few days.

E.   You validate Jason by saying, "Knowing how much your family means to you, I get how losing your dad has wrecked you. I am glad you've been so open with me. I'll figure out how to quit vaping, set a quit date, and talk to you about it."

Look at your answers to these three vignettes. If you answered any combination of letters, that's helpful to know. After a breakup, we don't move through these stages in a straight line. Grief can make us feel lots of different things at the same time as we are trying to make sense of it all.

If you answered mostly As, you're likely experiencing **denial**. You and your brain are not ready yet to deal with the unwanted news of a breakup. You are likely feeling numb and in shock. Being in denial can give you a little more time and space to come to grips with the change that's happening. During this time, it's important to make sure you nurture yourself and get plenty of rest, water, and nutritious foods.

If you answered mostly Bs, you're likely experiencing **anger**. It's normal to feel angry at your ex for what has happened and for all that you're suffering through. It can be helpful to acknowledge for yourself that it's okay to feel anger, which is an expected emotion after a breakup. It's important though to make sure that you aren't taking action or making decisions related to your ex from this angry place. See what decisions or actions can be put off until you've had a chance to calm down; for example, wait before you throw out gifts from your ex, hold off texting your ex for now, and avoid social media.

If you answered mostly Cs, you're likely experiencing **bargaining**. In the bargaining stage of grief in a breakup, you may be wishing for a second chance. You see the problems in the relationship more clearly, and you want to go back to the past and fix or change what has happened. You might promise yourself that you'll never check your ex's text messages again. Or you might change your mind and ask to undo the breakup. In this stage you may feel guilty, regretful, uneasy, uncertain, or agitated. As difficult as this stage can be, bargaining can help you sit and examine why the relationship didn't work, which can help your mind adjust to your new reality.

If you answered mostly Ds, you're likely experiencing **depression**. After you realize that bargaining didn't work, you go into the depression phase, which can be the most difficult stage of grief. This deep sadness is focused on feelings surrounding the loss and is a normal reaction to a breakup. You might feel hopeless, sad, or just not yourself. You might have difficulty eating, sleeping, or enjoying the activities you normally would. You may even ask yourself, Will I ever feel normal again? Even though it may feel like this stage will last forever, rest assured that it won't. In grief, it is normal to expect a dreadful day or bad moment, but it will eventually pass. In fact, none of the stages of grief after a breakup last forever. Your grief will likely jump around from stage to stage before finally settling into the final stage: acceptance.

> **NOTE:** If you have a history of depression or experience worrisome symptoms (feel depressed, have lost interest in things you care about or would normally enjoy, or find life to be meaningless), reach out to a mental health professional or your family doctor. Depression is treatable, often with ongoing counseling and sometimes with medication. Don't suffer alone.

If you answered mostly *Es*, you're likely experiencing **acceptance**. You're beginning to accept the reality of the end of your relationship. You may even be considering things in the relationship that didn't work for you, and you're starting to look at things differently. You're beginning to move past your pain and into the next phase of your life. You see that by being able to learn from the mistakes of the past and carry those lessons into your future, you can grow as an individual. You're ready to learn and thrive!

Grieving what was lost can help you begin the process of moving forward. Understanding your grief can help you shift from Will I ever get through this? to What can help me get through this? Let's review the common thoughts that come up in each of the five stages of grief.

- Denial: It's not really over.

- Anger: How could he do this to me?

- Bargaining: Maybe if I call her, we can stay friends.

- Depression: I'm never going to feel whole again.

- Acceptance: That really wasn't the best relationship for me.

Coming to terms with your relationship ending can leave you feeling out of control and in pain. You may be thinking Will I ever get over her? or Will this pain ever go away? Trust me, you'll learn to live without your ex, and you'll feel better. Let's look at the brain for an explanation.

The Neuroscience of Love

What happens in your brain when you have a romantic connection with someone? Neuroscience can help explain why we feel so connected to our partners and why it can be so hard to say goodbye.

All parts of the brain contain tiny cells called neurons. These cells carry messages, and when one neuron sends a message to another, a neural pathway is created. The more that pathway is used, the stronger it becomes. Think about it this way: When you spend time with your romantic partner, your brain creates thousands of neural pathways that become devoted to your partner and get stronger each moment you spend together. The feelings of connection activate the brain's *dopamine system*, which is the part of the brain that creates the strong desire or craving you feel for the other person. In a sense, your brain gets accustomed to being with that other person and will crave—or expect to keep getting—the usual rewards: physical touch, return of affection, emotional connection, and the like.

After a breakup, the neurons in your brain will keep firing as usual, as your brain seeks its reward of the neurochemical dopamine. Rewiring your brain to forget the rewards associated with your ex will take time. Until then, the cravings for your ex will continue. Remember, your brain is used to getting rewarded by seeing your ex and is going to do whatever it takes to activate the neural connections with your ex. Each time you contact or are contacted by your ex, look at pictures or old texts, or obsess over their social media, you're reactivating the neural pathways that are connected to your ex. From the viewpoint of neuroscience, couples who get back together after a breakup are seeking the dopamine reward and satisfying the urge for the familiar connection. It may seem that contacting your ex and hearing their voice will help you feel better, yet doing that can make it harder to learn to live without your ex.

The good news is that your brain is constantly learning new skills and rewiring its neural connections. This ability of your brain to learn and change throughout your lifetime is known as *neuroplasticity*. Think about when you learned something new, like playing a musical instrument, riding a bike, or even algebra. It was difficult at first, but it likely got easier over time. Let's use the metaphor of a train to further understand how neuroplasticity can help you have patience and consider your choices as you learn to live without your ex. Think of your brain as a train; the neural pathways are the train tracks, and you're the conductor. As you encounter or think of your ex, your brain (train) will automatically travel down the same neural pathway (train track) to seek the reward (dopamine) of familiar connection. Remember, each time you travel down this track toward your ex, the more that familiar neural pathway is used, and the tougher it will become to move away or disengage from.

Think about a time when you saw your ex after your breakup. How did it go? You may have gone over to talk to them one more time. While this may have felt good at first, this rush of excitement is temporary. Your brain, like all of ours, seeks to reestablish familiar connections with your ex to feel better (craving). Research has proven that a person can become addicted to love. Like any other addiction, a love addict will repeatedly turn toward unhealthy and painful relationships, often because of low self-worth, past trauma, or childhood issues (Mellody 2003). Romantic love causes the brain to release dopamine, the neurochemical that can lead a person to crave their ex much the way a person addicted to alcohol or drugs craves their next drink or fix.

Basically, as you continue to adjust to the loss of your relationship, your brain needs to catch up. Your brain will continue to crave the dopamine associated with your ex. The practice of *resisting the urge*, when you act in a new way toward something you normally crave, can help. An example would be to reduce or limit contact completely with your ex. This can be difficult, especially if your ex is reaching out to you or you see them on a regular basis. The more you practice not engaging with your ex, the easier it will be. You may need to tell your ex of your choice for no contact.

Let's look at the next Triangle of Change (TOC) to better understand the neuroscience of breakups. When you grieve, you're in pain, represented by the tip of the triangle. Each time you crave and reconnect with your ex (whether by text, meeting up, or even just imagining the two of you getting back together), the neural connections to your ex in your brain get reinforced with each dopamine rush. Remember, these reconnections are quick fixes; you won't feel better in the long run. It has been said that to truly heal from a breakup, you need to establish a life without your ex (Winch 2018). Therefore, each time you resist the urge to contact your ex, you're retraining your brain. As you breathe through to your steady footing on the bottom of this TOC, visualize resisting the urge: Yes, I can make changes. Each effort at this will balance your steady footing.

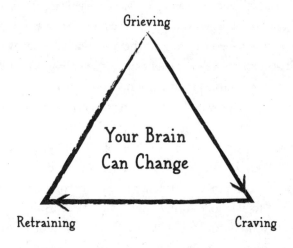

Find a New Path

As you continue to practice having no contact with your ex, the next step is to choose what to do instead. I call this the "when you feel out of whack, try a different track" coping skill. Try this: the next time you see your ex, you (the conductor) pump the brakes to slow down so you can see a different track to choose. Slowing down allows your brain to think first about your choices and then take a deliberate action.

Right now, you might be thinking that you can't even imagine a time when you won't think about or want to contact your ex. I get it. They were your go-to person for everything. For now, acknowledge that by choosing to do the opposite when it comes to your ex, you will eventually feel better. Try not to even talk about them; that can help too. Focusing on other parts of your life reinforces the truth that you're more than just someone going through a breakup. This refreshed perspective encourages hope that you won't always feel this bad. Responding to your ex in a new way, down a new track, will send new messages to your neurons. In time and with practice, your new neural pathways will become stronger, and your new actions easier. This is how you change how you think, feel, and act.

Let's Recap

This chapter acknowledged that your breakup likely impacted your daily routine, self-care, school performance, and other relationships. To help normalize the different feelings you're experiencing, you learned about the stages of grief after a breakup. It's common to focus only on the negative side of a situation. For example, you may be dwelling on all you've lost due to your breakup, yet making room for an alternative view can shed light on any silver linings, or hidden opportunities. With practice, thinking about your problems in this way can help you feel better in the moment and begin to work toward acceptance.

What strengths, resiliencies, or resources do you think this mindset can help you discover about yourself?

There's no easy way to figure out how to stop thinking about or wanting to see your ex. It's hard! I struggled very much with this part of my breakup recovery too. As you continue to accept the changes to your routine, understanding the neuroscience of love and cravings can help you think about your best interests. Remember, your brain has the power to learn and change, and so do you. In time, with patience and hope, you'll feel better and happy again!

SKILL 3

Prioritize and Nurture Yourself

Going through a breakup, whether it was a shock, a mutual decision, or your choice, can provoke all-consuming reactions. Memories of your ex are unavoidable and can surface anytime without warning. Your heart rate goes up. You may even feel anxiety-related nausea, which goes away after you calm down. This would happen to me, even while in college, when I returned to our hometown. My mind would race and all I could focus on was Will I run into him? or What if he ignores me? When and how these reminders happen is out of your control. What *is* in your control is how you react and how you talk to yourself about it.

Many people cope with their intense emotions by getting into behaviors that provide temporary relief, but at a great personal cost, for example, alcohol and drug use, overeating, self-injury, gambling, and excessive spending. As an alternative, and what this book offers, are coping skills that we can all learn and practice to deal with stress and crisis in healthier ways that make our lives better, not worse.

Let's explore healthy ways to adjust to your life without your ex. Make sure you're paying attention to your needs, both emotional and physical. Being mindful in the moment and managing distress are coping skills taught in dialectical behavior therapy (DBT), created by psychologist Marsha Linehan, that can help you understand and accept difficult feelings (Van Dijk 2021). First, DBT encourages you to observe your thoughts, feelings, and what you feel physically. For example, do you feel your heart rate speeding up when you're anxious? When you're angry, do you clench certain muscles in your body? By observing, you learn that thoughts, feelings, and physical sensations do indeed come and go, and as they do, they'll decrease in intensity. Next, DBT teaches that describing what you feel and do when you are anxious, angry, or upset helps you stay in the present and focus on what you can do to make things better. Like a singer who sings on the beat or a basketball player who effortlessly makes the layup, practice the coping skills discussed in this book often, even if you're not up to it. As I hope you will see, these skills can be enjoyable and not feel like work.

Later in this chapter, I'll be introducing another tool, the breakup reaction triangle, to help you gain control over your reactions and restore your calm. Using this triangle can help you start feeling better today!

How Are You Really Doing?

Let's talk about how you're holding up. The first few weeks, and even months, after a breakup can be a blur. Are you having problems at school, work, or home? Are you obsessing over your ex's social media? Has your sleep or appetite changed? These are common things that happen when emotions, not reasoning or thinking about consequences, control coping. The questions that follow can help you explore how you're coping with your breakup. You can download these questions, write your answers in your journal, or talk about them with a trusted adult. Remember, this is meant to help you move through your pain and toward healing. This is a *judgment-free zone*. Once you understand how you're coping, you can determine what is helping you to feel better and what is not.

- Are you keeping up with your usual self-care activities?

- Are you having problems with school (attendance, grades, focus)?

- Are you having problems with any of your other relationships (family, friends, classmates, teammates, coaches)?

- Are you sleeping more or less than usual? Are you having trouble falling asleep, or waking up in the middle of the night and unable to fall back to sleep? Are you restless throughout the night?

- Are you taking anything to help you sleep? If so, what is it?

- How is your appetite? Are you overeating? Restricting? Are you eating when you're experiencing emotions other than hunger?

- Are you engaging in any risky or out-of-control behaviors with drugs, alcohol, or unprotected sex?

Practicing regular self-care can help manage stress, boost energy, and improve mood. The way you treat yourself physically can affect your ability to manage or control your emotions, especially the intense ones. Spending too much time in bed, scrolling on your phone, or playing video games can mean you're stuck in your emotions. When you feel sorry for yourself, you may experience more problems. In contrast, research has shown that people who don't engage in a pity party are more likely to be mentally strong and recognize that self-pity can become a self-fulfilling prophecy (Morin 2014). Therefore, taking the time to practice self-care will not only help you get unstuck, but it can also help you live a more meaningful life.

How has your self-care been recently? Maybe you can't remember the last time you brushed your teeth or washed your face. Or perhaps you notice you're eating more or less than usual. Do you find yourself snacking without thought or awareness? Are you skipping meals on purpose or forgetting to eat? Sleep changes are normal too as you're adjusting to your breakup: sleeping too much, too little, or not at all. Neglecting these basics of self-care can make you feel worse, not better.

The good news is you can try to take small action steps today that can help ground you in the present, get back on track, and be motivated. For example, you could wash your face with a fresh-scented cleanser, plate up a healthy snack, or set a reminder on your phone to help you wind down to sleep. These actions can boost your spirit by helping you focus less on your worries, even if just for a bit. And you may feel better knowing you're doing things to take better care of yourself.

Mindfulness

Mindfulness is about being present in the moment, on purpose, and without judgment. When you choose to focus or concentrate on something specific in the moment, you're being mindful. Choosing to focus on an activity, your senses, or surroundings can help. Try it. On your next walk or car ride, observe and describe anything you see or hear. Or set a timer for the next five minutes and give your full attention to an activity, like cleaning an area of your room or listening to music. Fully immerse yourself in this exercise. When distractions or worrisome thoughts come up, simply refocus on whatever it is that you're doing.

Think now about using mindfulness when you experience a painful or difficult moment. How might it feel to see your ex flirting with someone new at school? It's so easy to get overwhelmed here! I totally get it. At times like these, practicing *mindful breathing* (intentionally focusing on your breathing and holding your attention there) is a must. Breathe in for three seconds, pause for three seconds, then breathe out for three seconds. I'm using a three-second count here to match the three-sided Triangle of Change used throughout this book. When you're still, even if for a few seconds, you give yourself a reset. There is an opportunity here. You can't stop their flirting, but you can use mindfulness to slow down your anxious thoughts and keep them from getting more out of control. The more you pay attention to your feelings in this way, the more you practice purposefully responding to stress. Let's look at Lenny's story to see how mindfulness helped him cope with his recent breakup.

• Lenny's Story

Lenny, age sixteen, and his girlfriend Joy, also sixteen, broke up three months ago. She wanted to date other people. Lenny has a history of depression and struggles at times keeping up with his chores and homework. Right after the breakup, Lenny seemed to be doing okay and was spending time with his friends. Over the recent weeks, though, Lenny has started to feel sad and lonely and has been staying mostly to himself. He hasn't been going out for runs as he normally likes to do and hasn't seen any friends.

Lenny's mom noticed that he had been home more, and she asked him how he was doing. He got mad at her for asking and immediately shut down the conversation by putting on his headphones. Later that night, Lenny decided to download the meditation app his friend uses. At first, meditation felt uncomfortable, but Lenny grew to like how it helped quiet the thoughts in his mind when he imagined Joy dating other people.

As Lenny began to use meditation more regularly, it reminded him of how he liked to go for a run, which also helped him not think about his worries. Lenny started to recognize the pattern: when he did an activity with purpose (meditation or going for a timed run), he felt better; when he isolated in his room, mindlessly scrolling on his phone, he felt worse.

Lenny spoke to his mom and shared his insights into how he could deal with stress, and talking about it felt good. He set two goals for himself: to start running again and to spend time with friends. He realized that when he balances alone time with connecting to others, he feels less sad.

Remember, whether you dwell on the past or overthink the future, your mind is likely wandering and judging. When you practice mindfulness, your thoughts tune in to what you're sensing in the present. You can do mindful activities alone or in a group. Here are some examples:

- Think of a word that seems calming or soothing, like "accept," "peace," or "relax." Gently repeat the word to yourself whenever you need a mental boost.

- Focus on your breathing; breathe in for three seconds, hold for three seconds, exhale for three seconds.

- Eat mindfully; taste and savor your next meal. What flavor stands out for you? Was the food too hot or too cold?

- Meditate. Download one of the many meditation apps that can help guide you through deep breathing techniques and guided imagery.

- Notice things around you. On your next bus ride to school, do you see any pretty flowers? Are there any dogs out for a walk?

- Participate. The next time you take a gym class, count along with the instructor as they guide the workout—1…2…3.

- Pay attention to what you hear. Listen to rain falling on the roof.

- Visualize. Think of positive, peaceful settings like a beautiful beach, a peaceful meadow, or a fresh snowfall.

Distress Tolerance Skills

DBT encourages the use of distress tolerance skills to manage stressful and crisis situations without making them worse. Let's say that since your breakup, you've stayed in bed most days, feeling so down and unmotivated. Distress tolerance would encourage you to change your emotions by doing the opposite of what you've been doing. How do you think you might feel if you got dressed and went outside, even if for a bit? You might think less about your breakup if you got to see your neighbor's cute dog. We will go into more detail about this DBT skill called opposite action and its benefits later in the book.

Self-soothing techniques are a type of distress tolerance that encourages focusing on your five senses (sight, smell, hearing, taste, and touch) to relax your mind and body. They can help you reset when your social battery is low or when you're overwhelmed by worry or judgments. These activities can be incorporated into your everyday routine. Examples of self-soothing behavior include

watching your favorite show (*sight*);

smelling a cup of your favorite hot tea (*smell*);

listening to relaxing music (*hearing*);

eating hot soup on a cold day (*taste*); and

taking a warm bubble bath (*touch*).

Make a list in your journal of the self-soothing behaviors you already use or ones you would like to try either today or over the next few days. You can look at this list for ideas:

watch a movie	go for a walk	listen to music
write or journal	call a friend	do a craft
go swimming	play with a pet	play an instrument
go hiking	go to the mall	bake cookies
play a game	read a book	play a sport
go for a run	take a long bath	wash your face
organize your desk	rearrange your room	draw or paint
do a jigsaw puzzle	play a video game	practice a hobby
play fetch with your dog	wash your car	empty the dishwasher
sort your socks	do laundry	take photographs
lift weights	go to the gym	sing out loud
go to the beach	make a lanyard bracelet	do yoga

Did you know that it can take the nervous system at least twenty minutes to return to baseline when a person feels upset or when their emotions feel out of control? In the previous chapter, we discussed how tuning in to and labeling your breakup emotions can prepare you to consciously choose what you do next, instead of reacting impulsively. Remember the train brain metaphor? As you respond to your ex in a new way, down a new train track, you send new messages to your neurons. In time and with practice, your new neural pathways become stronger, and your new actions become easier. This is how you can change how you think, feel, and act.

You cannot control how you may feel when you see your ex at school or around town. What you *can* control is what you say and do. Tell yourself, *Be in the know to go slow.* Moving slowly before you act encourages you to think first about consequences. Knowing that you can pump the brakes on your train brain—your reactions—is encouraging.

Being in the know works best when you can tune in to and rate the intensity of your feelings as you're feeling them. A straightforward way to describe feelings is with temperature ratings, such as *hot, warm,* or *chill.*

Hot emotional states may stem from feelings like rage, anger, fear, jealousy, guilt, shame, blame, exhaustion, or other strong emotions and can lead to big reactions (like yelling, punching, being aggressive, angry texting, or social media stalking). You may feel out of control, amped up, or upset. These out-of-control emotions can feel big and hard to manage in the moment, especially if there are reminders of your ex everywhere or if you run into your ex at your usual hangouts.

Warm emotional states signify that the intense energy of hot emotions is in the process of being downregulated to a cooler, calmer state, giving you a solid footing as represented by the bottom, more steady part of the breakup reaction triangle.

Chill emotional states are less influenced by feelings and are usually more rational and logical. Chill emotional states—like feeling bored, irritated, confused, or other less intense emotions—are less likely to cause you to react badly or spin out of control.

Think about some ways that you already get yourself to a chill emotional state. You may listen to music, FaceTime with a friend, or bake some cookies. You likely aren't feeling bored anymore, and you're likely not thinking about whatever it was that was causing you to feel irritated. You can try this the next time you feel anxious about something. Name your emotion—I'm anxious— and then shift your attention to something satisfying that can make you feel positive, like texting a friend or taking your dog for a walk.

Your Breakup Reaction Triangle of Change

Let's practice using your breakup reaction triangle to help you downregulate, or decrease, the intense energy of your hot emotions from where you feel out of control or amped up, to a cooler, calmer state where you have solid footing and will think through consequences before you take your next step. You can trace the downward flow of energy from hot to warm to chill using the TOC below, or you can draw your own breakup reaction triangle in your journal.

Start by thinking of a recent time when you saw your ex and said or did something that you later wished you hadn't. Identify the hot emotions you experienced, including your physical sensations, and what you were feeling and thinking. What am I feeling right now, and where am I on my breakup reaction triangle? You can respond with something like, I'm so upset! My shoulders are so tense, and I can't sit still. I have to call her to find out why she's doing this to me. I'm in my hot zone.

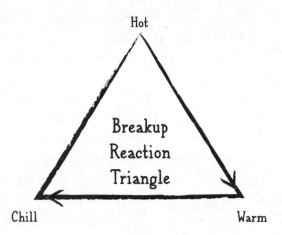

Using this triangle when you're dealing with a specific situation can help you practice accepting emotions in that moment. Accepting your situation as is doesn't mean you approve of it. Let's say that tonight is your friend's birthday party and you just heard that your ex will be there too. You can't believe he's still going. This is your friend group, not his. You rate your feelings as hot. You consider not going, but then you think about how that will disappoint your friend. Luckily you know a lot of people who will be at the party. You feel yourself becoming more chill, and you decide to go to the party after all.

In this example, accepting the situation (I can't stop my ex from going to the party) without fighting it allowed you to tune in to your emotions and problem solve. You are training your brain to slow down and consider your consequences and choices. Of course, this doesn't mean that seeing your ex at the party won't be difficult. It likely will be. If so, use your breakup reaction triangle to tune in to your feelings and consider what actions you can take to downregulate yourself to a more chill, steady footing. Thinking How do I want this to go? can help you move toward making a more conscious choice. Instead of reacting impulsively to seeing your ex at the party, quick-list your choices ahead of time:

- I can walk away.

- If I can't avoid eye contact or small talk, I'll keep it light and simple, talking about the newest movie or the new pizza place in town.

- I can nicely say that I'm here to see friends and would rather not talk tonight.

The good news is that by using a coping tool, like a breakup reaction triangle, you build a sense of confidence and competence in managing your emotions. By knowing the difference between your hot and cool breakup emotional states, you are preparing to cope more effectively when you need it the most. If you have a good idea that you may fly off the handle when you are heated up, knowing ahead of time what can help you cool down is priceless. Imagine being able to spend less time obsessing over your ex at the party and more time having a great time with your friends!

Being prepared, as this exercise shows, allows you to control your *amygdala*, the part of your brain that alerts you to a threat so that you can do or say something to protect yourself. Learning to resist the urge to react to your ex may be difficult depending on your relationship dynamic. Your brain may be trained to be on the defensive when you're around your ex, and this can make it harder to downregulate your breakup emotions. Explore your relationship with your ex in your journal to clarify how it makes you think about yourself.

- Write about a time during your recent romantic relationship when you were in a hot emotional state (for example, rage or jealousy). Did your partner do something that made you so mad?

- When you were in that state, what sort of things were you thinking about?

- If a stranger saw you when you were in a hot emotional state after a conflict with your recent romantic partner, how might they describe you?

- What's different for you when you're in a hot emotional state versus a chill one? What different physical sensations do you experience? Are your thoughts about yourself different or are they the same?

Zion's Story

Yesterday during school, Zion's girlfriend, Meghan, texted him that she wants to call it quits. She and her ex have been talking, and they are getting back together. Zion texted back asking if they could meet up after school to talk, and Meghan didn't respond. Zion was so distracted last night that he skipped basketball practice and got into an argument with his mother over not wanting to go to school the next day. Zion's mother asked what was going on and after several minutes he broke down in tears and yelled, "Leave me alone! Nothing ever goes my way." Zion's mother, seeing how upset he was, did not leave his room.

Finally, Zion noticed that he was getting angry at the wrong person. His mom was just trying to help. Realizing this helped him feel more chill and he told his mother, "I can't stop thinking about what went wrong." He admitted to not being able to focus on anything other than Meghan.

Zion and his mother talked about how he could cope when he overthinks about Meghan. They quick-listed ideas for things he could do to get his mind off Meghan, like talking to his teammates about their upcoming playoffs or getting caught up with his homework during study hall. Zion admitted to feeling a little better and less helpless now that he had some ideas for how to handle himself at school.

Zion's story demonstrates how his negative feelings (helplessness and worry) led to other hot emotions (anger) and his thinking negatively that nothing ever goes his way. After talking to his mother, Zion felt more in control of himself and was able to commit to returning to school. He has started to prepare to cope with the emotions that may come up when he sees Meghan. As

Zion continues to adjust to his breakup, his next step is to listen for any recurring themes of negative self-talk and counter them with more helpful self-talk.

Let's Recap

This chapter provided some ideas to help you shift your focus to things you can do to feel better, even if just for a little while. Doing things like going for a walk, practicing mindful breathing, or watching a dog run around playing fetch can help shift your focus to the present. This can be especially helpful during the early stage of your breakup, when your feelings may seem so overwhelming.

The breakup reaction triangle, a therapy tool, was introduced to encourage you to label your feelings as either hot, warm, or chill so that you can begin to feel the differences between each of these ratings. Once you're familiar with your different ratings, you can begin to choose which coping skill you need in that moment to downregulate, or decrease in intensity, your emotions. You may need to talk to a friend for support or not go somewhere if you're having a hot reaction (rage, jealousy, anger) to seeing your ex. In contrast, as you move toward a chill reaction (calm, accepting), you may not get too bothered, even knowing you may see your ex.

Part 2

HEAL

SKILL 4

Tame Your Critical Voice

Being in a relationship, whether it's long term or new, can make you feel special, worthy, relevant. The flip side, a breakup, whether by your own choosing or not, can be soul crushing, worrisome, isolating. As the shock fades, you enter the protest stage of your breakup, which can include anger, crying, yearning. This stage is when you come to terms with the reality of your loss, and it can last for many months. You may be consumed by thoughts of your ex and make attempts to reestablish contact. Research tells us that anxious individuals are more likely to suffer from *chronic mourning*—prolonged protest, despair, and continued attachment to their lost partner (Bowlby 1980).

The protest stage of a breakup affects your self-esteem, the degree to which you perceive your overall worth or abilities. Low self-esteem means having a poor opinion of yourself, and it can affect your sense of identity, belonging, confidence, and competence. One symptom of low self-esteem is *negative self-talk*, or using a pessimistic or unfair tone when speaking about yourself. For example, when I was freaked out about being single again, I blamed myself for being too needy. The healthier self-talk would have been for me to acknowledge both the parts of the relationship I could change and those not in my best interests. Believing in my abilities to make changes, knowing my worth, and trusting myself could have helped me. Instead, my low self-esteem strengthened an anxious attachment to my ex. I needed self-confidence to move away from negative self-talk, toward accepting and loving myself. Self-confidence is having the courage to believe in yourself, then acting on these beliefs. This is where we are heading!

What Is a Critical Voice?

Because your feelings, thoughts, and actions are interconnected, how you talk to yourself matters as it can affect your choices and behaviors. So how do you quiet your inner critic? Moving forward, we'll call this your *critical voice*, which by labeling brings attention to what it is—self-talk focused on criticisms, judgments, or disapproval regarding your own actions. This awareness doesn't mean that you agree with your critical voice; rather, it is the courage to make changes for yourself. You can tell that your critical voice is present when you judge or belittle yourself and it becomes difficult to think any other way. Let's look at a few examples of critical voice. Write in your journal any that you have said to yourself related to your breakup:

- I'm not good enough.

- I messed everything up.

- I lost everything that was good.

- I'm so stupid.

- I'm such a loser.

- I'm a bad person.

- Everyone will hate me.

- I never get anything right.

- Things never work out for me.

Much like anything, your critical voice can become a habit when it shows itself frequently. Habits can be hard to stop. Therefore, being aware of what your critical voice sounds like is the first step toward improving your self-esteem or worth (I'm good enough) and self-confidence or abilities (I can have a relationship with someone who gets me).

Hearing your critical voice in the moment is key to thinking more constructively about yourself and your abilities. The coping skill from earlier in this book, "Be in the know, go slow," can help here too. Know that your critical voice comes from somewhere. Unfortunately, you may have heard these negative things from either yourself or others. When something gets repeated enough times, you start to believe it. The skill here is to just hear your critical voice as it happens, and not believe it or act on it. Remember, even if you're thinking something, that doesn't mean it's true. Accepting that your critical voice exists will set you up for success here.

When you hear your critical voice (I'm unworthy of love), simply be aware of it and practice labeling (I'm having the thought that I'm unworthy of love). Essentially, this is how to quiet your critical voice. The more you label your thoughts as just thoughts, not facts, the more your brain will become familiar with your critical voice and the more comfortable separating from it. If you can, repeat out loud as many times as you want: I'm having the thought that I'm unworthy of love. Just because I'm thinking this doesn't mean it's true. Labeling a thought you're having as just a thought reminds you not to automatically believe it. I know this may be a new approach to your thoughts, and we'll continue to explore this skill, so you'll get more practice with it.

Don't Let Your Critical Voice Get the Best of You

We have established that your critical voice, if left on its own, will likely make you feel worse about yourself or your breakup. As you'll see later, a healthier alternative I like to call your *curious voice* can help quiet your inner critic by encouraging your self-awareness and growth. As you gain acceptance of yourself and your situation, yet another voice, your *compassionate voice*, will help you find balance, regulate your intense emotions, be mindful in the moment, and have better relationships.

Let's look at the next TOC to see where we are and where we're heading. Trace your finger along the TOC to help ground you. Start at the top point, breathing in. As you exhale, trace your finger along the side of the triangle from the top to the bottom right. Breathe in again, then exhale as you trace your finger down to the left corner. Visualize the downward flow of energy as you move away from your critical voice toward your curious and compassionate self-discovery. I hope you're starting to believe that you can build a more balanced and satisfying life.

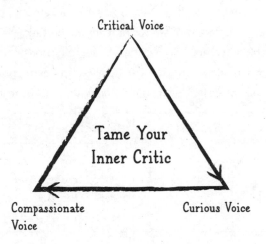

Cognitive reframing is a skill to help you shift your perspective by replacing flawed or negative thought patterns with more realistic or positive ones. Basically, it can help you think about a negative or challenging situation in a more positive way. The great thing about cognitive reframing is that you can practice it anywhere, anytime you're struggling. You can apply it to your view of yourself, others, situations, or relationships. This reframing could involve thinking about an upside to a negative event, or finding a lesson in a difficult situation. For example, as you shift your view of your breakup, you could think about the opportunities to meet new people, what you learned about yourself, and having gratitude for the time you spent with your ex. As you practice reframing your thinking, notice that your feelings and behaviors change too.

Adopting your curious voice can set you up to answer the question, What lesson is here for me? A curious voice can help you shift your focus from negative self-doubting to a more realistic acceptance of yourself. This is the path toward rebuilding your self-confidence after your breakup, and living a meaningful life again.

Let's take another look at common negative self-talk statements that may occur for teens during a breakup. Next to each is a reframe, or shifted statement, that reflects a more curious voice or realistic self-talk. As you look at this table, listen for the movement from critical voice to curious voice. The last two are intentionally left blank to give you some reframes to practice. You can download this table or write down your *Curious Voice* in your journal.

Critical Voice or Negative Self-Talk	Curious Voice or Realistic Self-Talk
I'm not good enough.	I have a lot of good qualities. I wonder what it was about our relationship that makes me feel less than.
I messed everything up.	I should consider why I do things like that and what I can do differently so I don't act like that again.
I lost everything that was good.	Yes, I have lost a lot because of my breakup. I still have other things in my life that are going okay, and it can help to remember that.
I'm so stupid.	Everyone messes up sometimes, even me. I know I'm not usually like that.

Critical Voice or Negative Self-Talk	Curious Voice or Realistic Self-Talk
I'm such a loser.	There were several reasons why we broke up. I'm already starting to see areas where I can improve.
I'm a bad person.	This was not an easy decision for me. I thought about whether we should break up for a while.
Everyone will hate me.	Some relationships end. I hope that in time people can understand that about us.
I never get anything right.	Mistakes happen, and I can learn from this.
Things never work out for me.	I've had tough times, but that doesn't mean that I always will.
I'll never get over this breakup.	I've gotten through plenty of bad things in the past. I can get through this too.
I never heard back from them. I must have done something wrong.	
I can't believe she did this to me. I'm never going to trust anyone again.	

Going forward, see if this reframing exercise helps you feel calmer as you practice shifting your mindset in a healthy way.

What Is Cognitive Behavioral Therapy?

Now that you have heard what your critical voice, or negative self-talk, can sound like, let's move to the next step: using facts to challenge your negative thoughts. Cognitive behavioral therapy (CBT) is a technique you can use to help handle everyday relationship challenges, as well as a range of intense feelings, such as anxiety, depression, anger, guilt, shame, blame, and low self-esteem. The premise of CBT is that your thoughts, feelings, and actions are interconnected and that if you change one of these, the other parts will change too. For example:

Today was a difficult day at school. You're overwhelmed with everything (feelings). You're struggling with wanting to FaceTime your ex (situation) to hear his voice. You think, I won't be able to get any homework done tonight. I'm such a loser (critical voice). You know if he doesn't answer, you'll feel worse and waste the whole night checking your phone for his response (fact).

Using a CBT model here can help you look at the information or facts you know to decide what to do next while considering your best interests. As you change the way you think about a situation, you also change how you feel and what you'll do. Let's look at the above scenario through a CBT lens:

You tell yourself it's okay to miss your ex and that a better idea would be to text your best friend (reframed thought). You feel better knowing you have someone else to talk to (feeling). You turn on your favorite background music that usually helps you do homework (behavior). You realize you're still upset, yet by shifting your perspective—acknowledging you have people to turn to for support and focusing on your needs and interests—you have made the situation more tolerable.

As you practice using CBT, I think you'll experience something very cool. You'll see that, in fact, you do have the power to change the way you think, feel, and act. And that by doing so, you'll feel better!

Look at the following TOC for one way to reinforce this skill. Trace your finger along the sides of the triangle and experience the prompts (reframe the thought, change the behavior, feel better) as building blocks toward healing. You can download this TOC or write it out in your journal, as well as a variation of the sequence (change the behavior, feel better, reframe the thought).

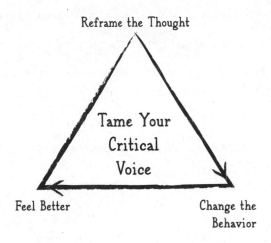

Are you starting to see how using CBT can have a positive effect on you? I really hope so. Remember, our goal here is to help you regulate intense emotions, find balance, and live a fulfilling life with your best interests as your guide. At this stage of your breakup, you could be getting used to life without your ex and learning to accept the reality of the things you've lost. You've probably shared your breakup story—how it happened, what you feel about it—many times. Being able to talk about your thoughts and feelings with others is a major step toward accepting things as they are instead of how you wished they were.

Let's continue to explore the CBT model to better understand the inter-connectedness of thoughts, feelings, and behaviors and the effect of our decisions on our whole being. The tools taught in CBT can help you think ahead about *consequences*, or responses that can occur. To practice, pick something related to your breakup that you want to process a little more. Maybe you just found out your ex is dating someone new, or it's going to be your first holiday season without your ex. Whatever the scenario, using the CBT model, ask yourself these questions:

- What recent situation affected me a lot? (activating event)

- How did my body react? (physical sensations)

- What did I tell myself during this situation? Where did I get stuck? (thoughts)

- What feeling or feelings did that thought lead to? (feelings)

- Did I experience a strong impulse to act? (urges)

- What did I do? (behaviors)

- What happened because of my behaviors or reactions? (consequences)

I hope this exercise was insightful and interesting for you. CBT can help you better understand yourself and have better relationships. Have you ever felt so out of control during an argument that you said things you regret? Do you ever feel like people don't understand you? When you practice using CBT, you'll gain skills that can honor who you are and what you need. By doing so, you can increase your self-esteem and your ability to build new relationships and take care of your existing ones.

Trisha's story can help you break down how thoughts and feelings can impact behaviors and consequences. It will show how using reframed thinking can help you act in your best interest and that of the other person.

• Trisha's Story

Trisha and Lisa were dating exclusively for six months during their senior year in high school. Lisa always wanted to see Trisha, even on days when they were both busy, and they spent a lot of time together. They were going to different colleges in the fall, and Trisha was sad about high school being nearly over. Her anxiety was through the roof lately. She worried all the time about having enough time and money to get herself ready for college by fall.

Their last big argument was right around graduation. Trisha wanted to spend time with her friend group, which Lisa was not part of. Lisa got really upset about this, so Trisha changed her plans to be with her. The week after graduation, Lisa kept texting Trisha asking her to hang out. Trisha avoided Lisa, not returning her calls, and leaving her Snaps unread. She knew ghosting Lisa was wrong, but she felt it was her only way to get some space.

As Lisa's texts and calls kept coming, Tricia, feeling overwhelmed, finally called back and abruptly broke up with her, yelling "I can't do this anymore! You're pushing me away by being too needy." Trisha ended the call without sharing with Lisa how anxious and sad she had been feeling lately.

Since her breakup, Trisha has been working a lot, not socializing, and snacking on junk foods at night when she gets home. Isolating and binge-eating are familiar to Trisha; they're what she's always done when her anxiety gets out of control. She's been to therapy in the past, yet she feels she doesn't have time for it right now. Trisha is feeling worse about herself and worries that she won't be ready to leave for college in a month.

Using the CBT model can help connect Trisha's thoughts and feelings to how she's coping with her breakup. Her decision to break up may have stayed the same; what might have changed is how she handled her breakup emotions, choices, and self-care.

Activating event: It's the summer before Trisha leaves to go away to college, and she's feeling overwhelmed and anxious all the time.

Thoughts: I really don't have enough time to dedicate to this relationship.

Feelings: Trisha is feeling overwhelmed, anxious, and sad.

Behaviors: Trisha first avoids Lisa. Triggered by Lisa's requests to see her, she then abruptly breaks up with her. Trisha copes by shutting down, over-focusing on work, and overeating.

Consequences: By falling back on behaviors she has struggled with in the past when she felt anxious and overwhelmed, Trisha is putting her health at risk. She feels unprepared to leave for college.

The work for Trisha is for her to connect her thoughts (I really don't have enough time to dedicate to this relationship) to her feelings (overwhelmed, anxious, sad) and her actions (avoiding Lisa, then shutting down).

What might have changed if Trisha had been able to connect her thoughts and feelings to her reactions? Perhaps if Trisha had shared her worries and sad feelings with Lisa, the two of them could have talked about their expectations for their summer before college. Each could have been a support rather than a stressor for the other. Had Trisha reframed her thought from less blaming (You're pushing me away by being too needy) to more constructive (I need some downtime to myself), she may have felt less overwhelmed and possibly been less prone to engage in unhealthy coping habits.

Common Breakup Thinking Traps

Congratulations on getting to this point. You've practiced the essential CBT skill of cognitive reframing. So, when do you use it? The short answer is any time you want to consider an alternative, more positive way to look at any given situation:

Reality: I have three tests all in one day tomorrow.

Cognitive reframe: I'll barely have any homework tomorrow night.

A more descriptive answer is to use reframing when your critical voice is overpowering you, like an obnoxious person talking so loudly at the movie theater that you can't hear the movie. When your critical voice takes over, what gets formed are *thinking traps*; negative thought patterns that aren't necessarily true and can be irrational. Calling them traps is helpful, as it reminds us that these are things to avoid. In this book, we'll focus specifically on what I call breakup thinking traps, or the exaggerated thoughts about your breakup that negatively impact your feelings and behaviors, and can possibly lead to anxiety or depression. As you start to notice these traps in your own self-talk, acknowledge them. Tell yourself, This isn't helpful or accurate. Good! This self-awareness is your building block to change.

Let's see what these traps are all about by looking at some of the common breakup ones:

Blaming: Viewing the other person as fully to blame for everything wrong in your relationship

Example: You're pushing me away by being too needy.

Catastrophizing: Overreacting to situations and believing the worst is going to happen

Example: I'm going to be alone forever.

All-or-Nothing Thinking: Thinking that things must turn out a certain way or else it's the worst thing ever; overlooking the possibility that things may lie on a continuum

Example: No one will ever understand me the way she did.

Idealizing: Remembering only the good things about your relationship and ignoring all the bad

Example: We were so happy; we barely had any issues.

Fortune Telling: Jumping to conclusions without having all the facts

Example: I won't ever be able to trust someone again.

Overgeneralizing: Thinking that just because something happens once, it will always continue to happen; regularly using words such as "always" or "never"

Example: I'll never be in a long-term relationship again.

Personalizing: Feeling that you're to blame for everything that's wrong in your relationship

Example: It was all my fault that we broke up.

Looking back at Trisha's story, what thinking trap do you think she was experiencing: (a) all-or-nothing thinking, (b) blaming, or (c) fortune telling?

If you answered *b*, you're correct. Trisha's thought (You're pushing me away by being too needy) drove many of her actions, both before and after graduation. She blamed Lisa for how she felt. Trisha's "it's all your fault" thinking kept her from considering her own feelings and behaviors. In contrast, had Trisha been able to talk about her vulnerabilities with Lisa, she may have felt less out of control and more able to make good self-care choices.

The next step after identifying any breakup thinking traps in your narrative is replacing them with more realistic or adaptive thoughts. To replace breakup thinking traps, first ask yourself any of the following:

- Is what I'm thinking even true?
- What evidence supports this?
- Does this thought serve me or not?
- Are there any assumptions present?
- Is there a different way for me to think about this?

Imagine asking yourself What evidence is there that I'll never be in a long-term relationship again? Shifting your viewpoint this way will make you happier, and your breakup thinking traps will be a thing of the past. Yay! We'll practice this skill in the next chapter.

Let's Recap

Thoughts are words that run through our minds. Thoughts are not facts. Just because you think I'll be alone forever or No one else will love me the way he did doesn't mean these statements are true. Thoughts are the things you tell yourself about what is going on around you. There are many ways to think about the same situation, some more helpful than others. When our thoughts are mostly negative or critical, we feel and act in unhelpful, even self-destructive, ways.

In essence, your critical voice, especially during a breakup, can keep you stuck in a painful emotional state. Knowing when you're stuck in a breakup thinking trap is your superpower moving forward. As you shift your self-talk from being less critical to being more curious, you give yourself the chance to think and feel more healthfully about yourself and your situation. Instead of I never get anything right, try Mistakes happen. I can learn from this.

Keep the Villains in the Movies

By now the reality of your breakup has likely hit hard. You're fully experiencing the void left by the loss of your relationship. You may be feeling at sea, without direction or purpose. Exhaustion, hopelessness, and maybe even a deep depression has set in. Known as the *disorganization stage*, this time represents the lowest part of the grief cycle. For me, my disorganization stage happened when I was in college. I remember feeling sad and aimless all the time. My extreme thinking—I'll never be happy again—was in overdrive. My behaviors mirrored my negativity. I skipped classes and kept to myself. I had forgotten my hopes and dreams—that I was in college to work hard and find a meaningful career while making memories and lifelong friendships.

While painful, this breakup stage is normal, expected, and necessary, as it lays the groundwork for your future self and relationships. Whatever your hopes and dreams, whatever is important to you, write them down in your journal and refer to them often. That's why you're here, to learn coping skills that will help you feel better and live a meaningful life. You deserve it!

Yes, your breakup took away so much and has left you feeling out of control or vulnerable. How you spent your time, likely your first and last texts each day, and the person you turned to when things weren't going well are all gone now. Not being with your person when you need them the most makes this stage of adjusting to your breakup so difficult. Trust me, having negative breakup feelings and thoughts is expected, and there is nothing wrong with you. It's from this exact place of disbelief and pain that you can learn about yourself and how you cope.

You feel good one minute, then start to cry uncontrollably the next. You function fine at school one day, and the next you dread being there and hear yourself coming up with ways to skip or leave. You find calmness in any glimmer of hope of getting back together, or you spend your time plotting your revenge. You worry so much about never feeling normal again that you start to believe you won't. Perhaps you badmouth your ex to anyone who will listen, or you speak so positively, hoping it gets back to them. You may spend your time alone so no one else can hurt you, or your schedule is jam-packed so there's no time to think about your ex.

These possibilities all make complete sense, given the changes you've gone through. Recognizing what is fueling these choices and actions can shed some light on how you react in times of emotional distress. As you move through this disorganization stage, you'll find your steady footing. To start, be curious and think about these questions:

- How did the relationship make me feel when it was thriving?

- How was it for me when the relationship wasn't working?

- How did I react when it was ending?

- How have things been for me lately?

Be Your Own Superhero

The goal of this chapter is to help you recognize the true villains here—your unhelpful breakup thoughts. They repeatedly pop up and try to control you. Much like movie villains who block the main character from finding happiness, your unhelpful thoughts will sneak up on you, ruin your day, and destroy your self-esteem. Remember, thoughts are just thoughts; thoughts are not facts. Just because you're thinking something doesn't mean it's true.

As these unhelpful thoughts get repeated over and over, they become stickier and more difficult to get away from. Think about it—the more you hear I'm going to be alone forever, the more likely you are to believe it. These villains become your automatic negative thoughts, the unhelpful lens you view everything through.

As the villains gain momentum, they become harder to ignore. You start to believe them as your absolute truth. What do you think your follow-up action might be? You may feel so unhappy that you turn down an invitation to hang out with a friend. You may even avoid doing the things that would usually bring you joy. As a result, you might find yourself alone, living out the thought, and reinforcing its effect: See, I'm all alone.

Of course, there are going to be times when saying no to an activity will be in your best interests. Staying home to recharge or take care of yourself is always a good idea. There is a difference between a self-care choice (I need to get caught up on things at home tonight) and a critical voice (They only invited me because they feel sorry for me). As you learn to be flexible and move toward a more realistic viewpoint, remember that your critical voice holds some self-awareness. Being self-aware means that you use your senses and experiences to better understand your emotions and to help you make conscious choices moving forward.

These questions can help you toward more helpful thinking:

- What are my thoughts about this problem or situation telling me?

- What part of this am I struggling with the most?

- How does this make me feel?

- What helped me in the past to feel better that I can do now?

- What small or gradual change can I make now?

Look at the following table. See if you can experience the down-regulated and more calming flow of energy as you move away from your critical voice (the villains) toward your more realistic, curious voice (the heroes). In your journal, set up two columns labeled as they are here, and practice reframing your thoughts this way. Your curious voice in this exercise intends to remind you that your negative self-statements are thoughts, not facts or absolute truths. If some of these pairs resonate more with you, you can add them to your journal. The more you practice thinking realistically (I'm having anxiety about this. This makes sense to me given all that I've been through), the less likely you'll believe your critical voice as your absolute truth. In doing so, you *extinguish*, or reduce the frequency of, your villains by replacing them with your heroes, the more realistic statements that acknowledge what you're going through.

The Villains: Your Critical Voice	The Heroes: Your Curious Voice
I'm going to be alone forever.	I keep thinking that I'm going to be alone forever.
I'm unlovable.	I keep thinking that I'm unlovable.
I'm not worthy of love.	I feel like I'm not worthy of love.
I made so many mistakes in my relationship.	I feel like I made so many mistakes in my relationship.
Everyone is going to hate me for breaking up with her.	I feel as if everyone is going to hate me for breaking up with her.
I'm broken.	I feel stressed thinking that I'm broken.
I won't be able to trust anyone ever again.	I'm thinking that I won't be able to trust anyone again.
I'm not good enough.	I'm feeling depressed about not being good enough.

Get Unstuck

Your villains—your critical voice—will cause you needless misery by being too rigid and confining. Moving away from seeing things in such extremes is how to get unstuck and finally break free from your villains. Recognizing when these villains appear is important. That's when you get to be your own super-hero. Picture it: as you hear the villains, you get to swoop in, superhero cape and all, and save yourself.

Move away from your critical voice and simply state what's happening (I keep thinking I'm going to be alone forever, or I keep thinking I'm so stupid). Remember, just because you're thinking something doesn't mean it's true. When you move away from the villains, they'll have less impact on you. To create distance between you and your villains, practice this skill every time you feel stuck. Hey, wearing a superhero cape can be fun. Enjoy!

Accept What You're Feeling

As noted earlier in this chapter, the disorganization stage, being the lowest part of the grief cycle, can be when hopelessness and deep depression can set in. This may sound like I'm worried that I'll never feel better or I'm so depressed and can be very discouraging.

Your feelings can be called out by naming them for what they are: hopelessness, depression, helplessness, frustration, fear, and so on (I'm having anxiety about this process or I'm feeling depressed about not being good enough). As you name your painful feelings, you're slowing them down and creating helpful distance between these feelings and what comes next. In essence, this distance encourages you to accept your feelings as they are, rather than having to change them. Remember, it's okay to not feel okay. As you accept what you're feeling, you allow yourself to feel your feelings (I'm having anxiety about being alone. It makes sense to me that I feel so anxious; a lot has changed for me).

To sum up this section, the more your critical voice gets repeated, the more likely it becomes a bad habit that is hard to shake off. In contrast, the more you practice and repeat helpful thoughts, the more you're training your brain to accept things as they are, not as you want them to be. Feeling down or frustrated about your situation is normal and necessary; it prepares you for figuring how to move through the next step.

Know When You Are Trapped

In the last chapter, you learned about seven common thinking traps that exist for any of us who have gone through a breakup; you can review them before going ahead. We've all been caught in one or more of those traps, and that's completely okay and normal. Hopefully you are recognizing, without self-criticism or judgment, the recurring themes of negative self-talk that you fall into from time to time.

Perhaps you've written in your journal or told a friend which of the common thinking traps come up often in your self-talk. Remember, just because you're thinking something doesn't make it true. By recognizing your unhelpful patterns as they pop up, you're listening to understand, not to judge yourself. The following example demonstrates how knowing when you're stuck in a breakup thinking trap can help you move from your critical voice to your compassionate voice.

Critical voice: Nothing ever works out for me.

Curious voice: I keep thinking that nothing ever works out for me. This is making me feel worse.

Compassionate voice: I do have some things that are going well for me right now. I raised my grade in chemistry, and I have plans to go out with friends on Friday. I need to not forget these things.

Next up, you'll learn specific coping skills that can train your brain to move away from sticky thoughts toward more factual ones.

Retrain Your Thoughts

When you hear your breakup thinking traps in your self-talk, you can consciously use coping skills to challenge them and get relief. CBT will help you again here. Remember, CBT teaches us that our thoughts, feelings, and behaviors are connected; each impacts the other. In CBT, we use *adaptive thinking strategies*, which are ways to challenge or reframe our negative thoughts. With practice, using adaptive thinking strategies trains your brain to think about things from a fact-based, more rational viewpoint.

You'll know you're using this coping skill when your thoughts become clearer and more rational than they usually are or have recently been. Being able to bend your thinking in this way, or having *cognitive flexibility*, as it's called, means you can hear the difference between your unhelpful, rigid sticky thoughts and your reframed, rational ones.

Let's look at the seven common adaptive thinking strategies in the context of breaking up:

Self-awareness: Seeing the reality of your breakup as having been affected by choices and actions by both you and your ex

De-catastrophizing: Thinking about how likely it is that your worst-case scenario will come true

Thinking in shades of gray: Knowing that things are rarely all bad or good, all success or failure; finding the middle ground

Examining the evidence: Weighing the evidence for your interpretation of your relationship with your ex

Putting into perspective: Seeing the true value or importance of something by comparing it to something else

Being specific: Sticking with the reality of your situation and avoiding judging yourself or your situation

Acceptance: Thinking about your breakup flexibly and in different ways, finding your truths, and accepting them

Now let's put this all together. As you hear your critical voice pop up with thinking traps, acknowledge them, but don't judge them. Instead, be curious: Is this a helpful thought for me right now? This curious mindset is your superpower here. It gives you both the thinking and the feeling skills to know when your thoughts are unhelpful and need to be challenged and reframed. Essentially, your curious voice will fuel your self-love and compassion: Yes, I'm feeling vulnerable. It makes sense to me, given all that has changed.

Practice Makes Progress

My hope for you is that, as you practice, being curious about what is in your best interest will become your new way of life. Let's look at the next Triangle of Change (TOC), called Practice Makes Progress, to experience the downward flow of energy as you move from being critical to being curious and compassionate. This TOC is a grounding technique that can help you downregulate your emotions from feeling out of control or amped up toward feeling cooler with a steady footing.

Critical Voice

Practice Makes Progess

Compassionate Voice

Curious Voice

Looking at this TOC, trace your finger following the downward flow of energy starting at the top point, where your critical voice exists. As you move down the right side, your curious voice guides you to think things through in a conscious and steady way. Experience how your mind and body are connecting right now as your voice becomes more compassionate, self-loving, and accepting of yourself and your situation.

The more you practice retraining your thoughts and using your curious voice, the better you'll get at it, and the sooner you'll feel relief. Just the way you repeat your layup in basketball, or your pirouette in ballet, you practice until you get it right. The same holds true in changing your thinking to be more self-loving and accepting. The more you retrain your thoughts, the stronger your compassionate voice (the kinder, more self-loving way to think about yourself) will become. The more you hear your compassionate voice, the resulting steadier footing will reinforce how calming it feels, making this a new habit for you. With regular use, your refreshed compassionate voice will become your go-to way to handle emotional distress.

Next let's look at the flow of energy with the help of the arrows as you practice using *adaptive thinking strategies* to ignite your compassionate voice. In each example, notice the shift in voice as it progresses from "breakup thinking" to "adaptive thinking" to "retraining your thoughts."

To stop **blaming** yourself, try **self-awareness.**

Example: I pushed him away by being too needy. → Both of us had a part in this relationship, when it worked and when it didn't. I can also see that our breakup was messy and we both had a part in that too. → I want to learn more about my part in it to help me better understand myself.

To stop **catastrophizing,** try **de-catastrophizing.**

Example: I'm going to be alone forever. → My worry over being alone forever is just that, a worry thought. It isn't based on fact. → I'm a likeable person; it's quite likely I'll find another romantic interest in my future.

To stop **using all-or-nothing thinking,** try **thinking in shades of gray.**

Example: I'm a bad person. ➔ Yes, I made some mistakes in the relationship, and there are things that I did well too. ➔ I feel like a bad person at this moment, but I'm actually a complex person.

To stop **idealizing,** try **examining the evidence.**

Example: We were so happy; we barely had any issues. ➔ It can be helpful for me to look at what parts of the relationship I miss, and what parts didn't work for me so well. ➔ I want to remember my relationship with my ex with a clear head so I can consider all the things that led to our breakup.

To stop **fortune telling,** try **putting the situation into perspective.**

Example: I won't ever be able to trust someone again. ➔ My trust has been broken. Looking at how I dealt with being hurt and losing trust in past relationships can help me. ➔ I have maintained trusting relationships with several friends and family. In time, I'll trust a romantic partner again.

To stop **overgeneralizing,** try **being specific.**

Example: I'll never fall in love again. ➔ I do like being in a romantic relationship, so in time, this is something I'll want again. ➔ I can think about the opportunities to meet new people and the things I learned from the relationship.

To stop **personalizing,** try **acceptance.**

Example: It was all my fault that we broke up. ➔ I'm ready to accept my role in our breakup. This acceptance can help me learn more about myself and why I react to things in certain ways. ➔ Sure, I made mistakes, but realistically we both did. I can take responsibility for myself so I can heal.

To practice using adaptive thinking strategies, let's read about Sheila's recent breakup. Listen for where Sheila's thinking gets trapped.

• Sheila's Story

Sheila broke up with her girlfriend, Kelly, after being together for six months. They had been fighting a lot toward the end of their relationship, spending hours arguing on the phone every night. Sheila was busy applying for a summer internship, and she couldn't deal with all the time it took to deal with their issues. Needing relief, she decided to break things off, thinking it would be better for both of them.

Since their breakup, Kelly has been very upset at school and has often been seen crying. Most of their friend group seem to be ignoring Sheila and spending all their time consoling Kelly. Feeling left out and unsure how to react, Sheila started to skip school. When she realized that her sleep and grades were being affected, Sheila decided to go back to school and talk to her guidance counselor. Sheila told her counselor, "I've lost my entire friend group forever."

There can be several ways Sheila is thinking about herself and her situation. Is she jumping to conclusions? When she says that she has lost her friend group forever, is she fortune telling?

Thinking about Sheila's story, which breakup thinking trap is present for her? You can write your ideas in your journal. Make sure to focus on your reasoning and what you would say to Sheila to help her realize that her thoughts and reactions are trapping her and not helping her move forward.

Next, name the adaptive thinking strategy that can help her get unstuck and focus on the facts. If Sheila were your friend or sister, what might you say to help her? What adaptive thinking strategy, or curious way to think, would you encourage her to try? Might putting her situation into perspective help Sheila? How?

Let's Recap

Simply put, your breakup is going to make you think and feel lots of different things. The villains, or unhelpful negative thoughts, will sneak up on you from time to time. As these villainous thoughts get repeated, they become more difficult to ignore, and they will trap you. Knowing when you're stuck in a breakup thinking trap can help.

Tuning in to your thoughts, feelings, or urges means you become fully aware of them without judging them. This practice of self-care encourages you to feel, think things through, and consider your choices. Giving yourself this time to process and think about your best interests helps you validate and accept your experience as it's happening. As you do this more often, you'll better understand your triggers and how you cope, and you'll become more self-loving.

SKILL 6

Ask Curious Questions

Even though you may be back to your regular routine, that doesn't mean you're back to being okay. Whether you were the one who initiated the breakup or not, your self-esteem may still feel wrecked. Maybe you said or did things at a party or on social media that you wished you hadn't. Perhaps you're now the only one of your friends without a prom date. Yes, these things can sting. My ex moved on with someone new before I did, and instead of seeing this as natural, it worsened my outlook. What I needed was a perspective shift that would encourage me to focus less on my past and more on my future.

We've explored strategies to help you regulate emotions and practice being present. Specifically, the skills taught have encouraged you to observe, pause, and downregulate intense breakup emotions to a cooler mindset. Finding your balance, your calm and steady place, has been the goal. Understanding what your critical voice sounds like has formed a solid foundation to help you make changes. Your critical voice can reveal your hidden, harder-to-manage vulnerabilities. Figuring out what these are is where we're going here. Being curious can help you answer these questions:

- What are my emotions telling me?

- What have I been struggling with lately?

- Have I been more irritated or down than usual?

- Have I stopped doing the things I usually enjoy?

Accepting the reality of your breakup doesn't mean you will, or have to, agree with the circumstances. Although you may still get angry or depressed about it, the insight you can gain by asking yourself thought-provoking questions will help you move through your pain toward acceptance and self-love. Being curious can help you consider solutions: What is in my best interests right now? or What choices do I have?

Accepting Reality

To accept things as they are, not as you want them to be, means being aware that your negative thoughts are just thoughts, not facts. Think about the last time you heard yourself thinking This isn't fair or I can't get over this. These thoughts likely made you feel worse. When you fight reality in this way, the pain of your negative beliefs or feelings will intensify. If you keep saying I can't get over this, you're going to believe that there really is no way out of your painful situation.

As difficult as this has been, your breakup happened for a reason. And yes, sometimes the reason given can be frustratingly vague. Whether you were the one who heard "It's not you, it's me," or the one who said it, the breakup still happened. Replaying the circumstances surrounding your breakup will keep you stuck. Trying to piece together information will likely not give answers, and will add fuel to the blaming, shaming, and guilt train. The better way to put the pieces of your life back together is with self-love, understanding, and using coping skills. This way, you get to love your life again and become the wiser version of yourself, better able to withstand intensity and pain.

Look at the following table to help you think about this idea. As you follow each row from left to right, see if your energy shifts from feeling invalidated to feeling encouraged, even hopeful. If it doesn't, that's okay. The more you practice the exercises in this book, the more they'll become your go-to mindset.

Write the statements in your journal that best apply to you, making sure to include both statements from the left and right columns to help you feel the shift in your energy—from fighting your reality toward a calmer, more accepting mindset. You can use the last two rows to come up with your own ideas for accepting reality.

Fighting Reality	Accepting Reality
This isn't fair.	This is difficult.
Everything feels out of my control.	I can focus on small things that I can control, like when I shower or when I start my homework.
Nothing ever works out for me.	I'm struggling to get over this.
It shouldn't be this way.	This may take a while for me to get used to.
I can't deal with this.	I'm starting to be okay with parts of my life without him.
I can't accept that this has happened.	I'm getting used to the idea of being single again.
I can't get all this homework done.	I'm starting to get caught up with my missing assignments.
Everyone hates me.	My support system has changed, but my close friends have stuck by me.
It is going to take me forever to get over my ex.	
I should just keep reaching out to them so they feel obligated to respond.	

Accept and Allow

How did it feel for you to work on that exercise? Maybe it felt natural to go from left to right on the table to hear yourself repeat the accepting reality statements. Maybe it didn't. It can be a difficult exercise to complete. *Accept and allow* refers to changing your mindset toward unpleasant thoughts so that they lose their power and start to feel like ordinary thoughts (Winston and Seif 2017). So, if you hear yourself say It's taking me forever to get over him, recognize that your emotions are telling you something. Maybe you're exhausted or frustrated that your favorite season just passed and you barely enjoyed anything.

It can help to repeat out loud the accepting reality statements to become more comfortable with shifting your mindset in this way. You can also select a few of these statements that most resonate with you, or you can use your own. As you repeat each statement and hear it out loud, you're training your brain to accept the statement as is, even if you don't like it.

By just letting the statement be, rather than pushing it away, you allow yourself to be at peace with it. For example, by accepting that I'm struggling to get over this, you can then acknowledge Of course this is hard; I was really in love with my ex, and hopefully feel validated. This acceptance offers a steady footing to help make emotional pain more tolerable as you continue to process what you're going through.

Instead of getting annoyed with yourself by focusing on how long it's taking you to get over your ex, try validating how challenging this process has been and that you're doing a good job. What's the key lesson here? When you fight and resist your thoughts, they will persist and stay stuck. Instead, if you accept and allow the process you're in, you'll be less upset and better able focus on healing.

What If I'm Making Unhealthy Choices?

Try naming something you recently did that you're unhappy about. This awareness could signal that you're fighting the reality of your breakup. Maybe you're sleeping more than usual, using drugs or alcohol to escape, or lashing out at others. It can be helpful to think about how you've been expressing your breakup emotions. Perhaps your family or friends have been telling you that you've been difficult to get along with or that you seem on edge lately. If so, how was it for you to hear such feedback? The work here is to ask yourself the following questions to see what your breakup emotions are telling you. I encourage you to download these questions or write out the questions and your answers in your journal, starting with today's date, and then complete them each week to see your progress.

- When things don't go right for me, how do I handle it? Do I shut down? Lash out at others?

- Have I been using my breakup as an excuse for any recent behaviors?

- Have I been relying on alcohol or drugs to help me cope?

- Have I been avoiding any of my responsibilities, either at home or at school?

How Vulnerability Can Help You Thrive

I hope that you're starting to see how being curious can help you become comfortable with accepting reality. A curious voice can sound like: I'm struggling right now, which makes sense to me given all that's changed. Remember, your curious voice is your reality-based lens to assess your own thoughts, feelings, and beliefs, to see how you're doing. Having an awareness of what's helping or what's getting in the way of finding your steady ground can rebuild confidence.

While being vulnerable isn't easy, it can boost your confidence and belief in your ability to handle challenging situations. This growth can make you more resilient in the face of life's challenges. Say, for example, you sometimes say or do things you regret afterward. Knowing why you got triggered and being able to speak to it is a great way to grow. Research has shown that accepting our own vulnerability is a measure of courage that benefits ourselves and our relationships (Brown 2017). Examples of vulnerability include the following:

- Feeling difficult emotions such as shame, anger, or fear

- Talking about mistakes you've made

- Sharing personal details with people you trust that you normally keep private

- Taking chances that might lead to feeling disappointed

- Reconnecting with someone you've lost touch with

- Being honest about what you need in a relationship, including your boundaries, expectations, and hopes

- Trusting someone again

- Saying yes to things that you enjoy doing and had recently stopped doing

Let's look at Jayson's breakup to understand how his vulnerabilities show up.

• Jayson's Story

Jayson's girlfriend, Elena, recently broke up with him because she wanted to date other people. When anyone asks how he's doing, he says he's fine and quickly changes the conversation. He doesn't want people to see him upset. Jayson remembers that when he was younger, his father called him weak for crying over losing his favorite toy.

Since the breakup, Jayson has been staying up late playing video games, and his mom must ask him several times to do anything. During their last argument, he yelled at his mom to stop making demands on him. Feeling frustrated and overwhelmed, Jayson recently started smoking marijuana with a friend after school.

What vulnerability is coming up for Jayson? My thoughts are that he seems uncomfortable talking about his feelings and is using avoidance behaviors (playing video games and smoking marijuana) to cope. The better choice for Jayson would be to consider a time when he asked for help and felt better. Maybe it was for something he was motivated about, like asking a teacher for an extra-credit assignment to improve a grade. Jayson's curious question could be: How was it for me to ask for help that time? He may connect that it was uncomfortable at first but that he's glad he asked. Ah! Bringing vulnerabilities into awareness like this can help guide, not block you. This sure sounds very self-loving to me.

Pause, Pivot, Shine

When I'm challenged by a difficult situation and deciding what to do next, my favorite coping skill, the **pause**, can be a game changer. It might be one for you too! When you press the pause button (as I like to call it), you give yourself an invaluable moment to breathe in and out before anything else. Pausing gives your feelings a chance to come down in intensity from hot to cool so you can be more skilled at managing your urges and impulses to react. The pause button enables you to make an intentional choice about what to do next.

Pausing gives your mind and body a chance to get in sync. It lets you tune in to what you're feeling in that moment. Even just a few seconds can make a difference. Pausing trains your brain to be curious and ask yourself, How do I want this to go? What choices do I have? What's my best choice?

When you pause, you acknowledge I can think this through, or I can control my reactions. Remember that earlier we talked about your brain being like a train? You have two tracks to choose from. Visualize the pause button as the brake on the train. Before you release the brake to get moving, consider which track is best for you. Being able to **pivot** here means you've taken stock of what's going on in your present moment. Based on this information, you choose what to do next. The idea of a pivot, in live time, is to quickly think, I have choices here; which one works best for me right now?

Sometimes it's clearer than other times to know when to pivot. Say, for example, you and your ex are in the same ELA class. Knowing this can help you prepare ahead of time. You might think, I'm anxious about seeing my ex next period. I'll get to class a little early so I can get settled at my desk.

In contrast, unexpectedly running into your ex and their new partner at a local coffee shop can throw you off balance. Feeling anxious, you pause to consider your choices: to react or not. You pivot toward the path of being gracious, smiling at them both as you exit the coffee shop with your mocha cappuccino in hand.

With practice, being able to pivot in the moment will help you handle stress as it comes up. Imagine how you might feel as you handle life in this way, with steady footing and self-love. Your compassionate voice will speak up regularly for sure: I really like how I handled myself in that situation. It was tough at first, but I worked through it.

My hope is that you're feeling more encouraged about reflecting on your vulnerabilities. This refreshed mindset can help you change the way you see things, to feel calmer and more accepting of yourself. Knowing your vulnerabilities or underlying hurt feelings can help your self-love **shine** with acceptance as you tell yourself, It makes sense to me why I reacted that way. This book intends to help you form a new habit of being less self-critical and more self-loving.

Let's put this all together using the following Triangle of Change. You'll start at the top point of the TOC, move down the right side and out to the left to the more desired solid footing.

Pause when you hear your critical voice: I'm unworthy of love.

Breathe mindfully as you downregulate your feelings from hot to cool.

Pivot to your curious voice. What facts support this thought?

Shine as you experience your compassionate voice: *I recognize that this thought comes from past relationships.* Just because I'm thinking it doesn't mean it's true.

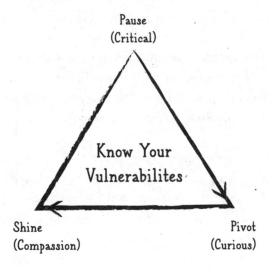

Pause
(Critical)

Know Your
Vulnerabilites

Shine
(Compassion)

Pivot
(Curious)

As you read the following statements, notice the flow of energy from feeling charged up or negative toward feeling calmer and more self-aware.

I can't believe I did that (critical). What else might have affected our breakup (curious)? I understand that my thoughts and actions are in my control (compassionate).

I'll never get over this (critical). What would be the worst possible outcome if this thought were true (curious)? I've worked through similar pain in my past (compassionate).

He never loved me (critical). Why am I questioning what we had (curious)? I'll find some ways to view this in a positive way (compassionate).

I could have done more to make it work (critical). Is there a different way to look at this same situation (curious)? I can see areas where I can make some changes (compassionate).

I'm so unlucky in love (critical). What am I willing to accept about my situation (curious)? I do see some benefits to accepting my part in my relationship ending (compassionate).

Maybe this means they want me back (critical). What evidence is there for that (curious)? I've become more comfortable looking for evidence that backs up the facts of how things are (compassionate).

I wonder if we'll ever get back together (critical). Would getting back together be in my best interests (curious)? I'll try to notice thoughts like this that get in the way of my accepting the reality of my relationship, not how I wish it were (compassionate).

I can't stop thinking about what they are doing (critical). How might I feel if I reach out and they don't respond (curious)? I'll try to notice thoughts like this that are getting in my way (compassionate).

Nothing good came out of my relationship with them (critical). Is there any way I might view this in a positive way (curious)? I'll practice thinking in shades of gray to help me see things as not all good or all bad (compassionate).

Boldly Go into Your Relationship Story

Becoming more familiar with your past vulnerabilities and wounds will give you a clear understanding of what you need and desire in your relationships, including romantic ones. You'll be able to speak about what works for you, what doesn't, and what makes you feel supported and heard. Your curious voice helps you better understand yourself so that your compassionate, self-loving voice can shine: I'm beginning to understand what I need in my relationships, and I'm getting more comfortable talking about this.

Overthinking and self-doubting, while common, can be incredibly draining and misguided, blocking you from seeing things as they need to be seen. Digging deep into how your relationship made you feel can bring into awareness the hard-to-talk-about stuff. Maybe you got jealous when your ex was out with his friends and didn't text you, because it reminded you of when you felt left out in the past. Perhaps you minimized the effect of your ex's cheating because it brought up too much pain from your parents' bitter divorce. Maybe you blame yourself when things don't work out for you.

As you continue to navigate your breakup, the goal is to move toward rediscovering yourself. Your curious voice can help by asking gentle questions to see what your emotions are telling you. Being able to speak about your vulnerabilities (where you get stuck) is how you gain self-awareness (what works for you and what doesn't).

The following list of curious questions can help you become more self-loving. They are broken down into four categories: self-awareness, relationships, coping, and negative thinking. You can download the list or write the questions and your answers in your journal. May this exercise help your outlook be compassionate and hopeful!

Self-Awareness

When do I feel most vulnerable?

What do I do when I feel vulnerable?

Have I recently felt unworthy? Unsafe? Rejected or undesired?

What could I have done better today?

What have I improved upon since yesterday?

Relationships

What do I value in my relationships?

Am I able to set boundaries in my relationships?

Do I speak about the things I need in my relationships?

How have I handled recent social situations that made me uncomfortable?

Coping

What happens to me when I feel uncomfortable?

Why do I think I respond in these ways?

What unhealthy choices have I made recently?

What changes do I want to make?

What changes do I need to make?

Negative Thinking

What facts support what I'm thinking about right now?

Is there a different way to look at this same situation?

What would the worst-case scenario be if this thought were to come true?

Am I overgeneralizing from a past experience to my present situation?

Am I giving myself the same kindness that I would show a friend going through a breakup?

If you felt uncomfortable as you answered these questions, that's okay. Thinking about past or current hurts can be hard. You may even have skipped over some questions, and that's okay too. The goal here isn't to make you uncomfortable, it's to help you be aware of how your past experiences showed up in your relationship with your ex. For example, you might wonder why you tolerated your ex belittling you and then realize that your dad often shames your mom, so it's familiar to you. Seeing things more clearly—why you get stuck, what you need, and how you want things to be—encourages you to think about solutions. I feel good knowing more about myself or I can focus on doing things that will help me feel better. Understanding yourself better is within your control and can help you in all your relationships.

Communicating Your Needs

While you cannot change how other people think, act, say, or feel, you can change how you react to them and how you communicate your needs. For example, if you constantly argued with your ex, demanding that they be more loving and affectionate, this way of communicating likely didn't help. In contrast, sharing with your partner the reasons why love and affection are important for you may not change things either, but it can lessen the tension between you two. Communicating in this way takes practice and can be hard to do if you're consumed by feelings or intense emotions.

To better understand your communication style, it's important to consider how your emotions show up in your relationships. Especially in romantic relationships, emotions can get very charged, making it difficult to communicate clearly. Have you ever spent all your time with your ex arguing over how you want to see them more? (I'm nodding my head in agreement as I write this. I totally get it.) Or when things were going well, did you dwell on the future of your relationship? (Here I am, nodding again.) If so, your anxiety may have been in overdrive and not letting you use your pause button. Pausing can help you slow down, make the connections as to why you're feeling the way you do, and then share it clearly with your partner. Knowing your vulnerabilities here can help make you feel less anxious as well as giving you insights into what you need from a romantic partner.

As you move toward rediscovering yourself, the benefits of knowing your vulnerabilities will become clearer. Yes, you'll get better at knowing when and why you're stuck or hurting. This will improve how you relate and communicate to others. You'll also become better attuned to which types of relationships suit you and which don't. Say you notice, as in the previous example, that your dad frequently shames your mom, and while familiar, this is not okay for you. Consider this: How comfortable were you sharing your expectations with your ex? Did you feel comfortable enough to talk about your problems? Having this sense of closeness in a relationship takes time and awareness.

Having a sense of closeness and openness in a relationship is related to the degree of intimacy between two people. The following questions relate to the four common types of intimacy found in teen romantic relationships: emotional, mental, spiritual, and physical. Which intimacy statements could describe your relationship with your ex? It can also be helpful to pay attention to which statements help you feel supported and connected in your relationships, especially your romantic ones.

Emotional

Was I able to share my deepest fears, pains, and doubts?

Was I able to take risks and be open?

Did I avoid outward conflict at all costs?

Was our fighting out of control?

Was I supported and comforted when I needed it?

Did I make choices for myself that were consistent with my values?

Mental

Did I feel safe expressing my own views?

Was I able to make choices on my own?

Was there abuse or coercion involved in my making choices?

What parts of the relationship do I wish had been different?

Could I speak freely, or was I threatened in any way that made me nervous or scared to talk?

When my partner and I had different views, did I feel respected or put down?

Spiritual

Was my spirituality supported in this relationship?

Was I able to speak freely about my spiritual practices even if we had different ones?

Was I belittled or encouraged when I spoke about my views on spirituality?

Physical

Could I have an open conversation about my level of comfort with different types of touch?

Were my boundaries and reactions respected?

Did we have enough time together to nourish our connection?

Was there any substance abuse or other out-of-control behaviors?

Looking at the wellness of your relationship intimacy, or connection, can help you accept the reality of what was and what wasn't in your best interests.

Let's Recap

In essence, being curious can help you hear what your emotions are telling you so you can better understand yourself and make choices that are more self-loving and in your best interests. You are likely still working through the disorganization stage of your breakup, when feeling aimless and hopeless is normal. Remember, just because you feel this way now doesn't mean you always will. It's my hope that you're starting to see you have choices to help you cope and feel better.

Even if you still feel bad, trust me, you're getting through this. There's no timeline or quick fix for getting over a breakup. Changes are more often gradual than dramatic. Perhaps you're starting to do more. Maybe you've been going for a walk when you feel down, or reaching out to family or friends when you feel lonely. Or you're trying new things or thinking in a new way. You may be considering things you would do differently or not put up with in your next relationship. You are jump-starting the change process. Great!

Part 3

SHINE

Sit with Your Discomfort

Let's check in on where you're at. The disorganization stage of your breakup may still be going strong and giving you rough days, sleepless nights, or constant *ruminating* (repeatedly thinking about or seeking solutions without success over a long period of time). Would we have stayed together if I had been more chill? Was breaking up the right thing to do? Will I ever be in a healthy relationship? Being on the Ferris wheel of never-ending self-loathing and self-doubt is awful. To make things worse, your mind is trying to convince you to believe things that aren't true. These misperceptions, or *cognitive distortions*, lead to unhealthy self-criticism and judgments.

After my breakup, I needed to press pause and get off the Ferris wheel of blame and shame. My vulnerabilities were surfacing, and I didn't like that. I felt helpless and unworthy. I sought constant reassurance from others, asking them to tell me that things would get better. While I may have felt better, that feeling was temporary. I wasn't learning how to nurture myself. What I needed was to find my solid ground, away from the cycle of rumination. This is my wish for you to create your steady footing, make constructive choices, and nourish your reality-based, self-accepting, and compassionate voice.

To review, thoughts can either help or get in the way of your breakup recovery. Specifically, when a negative thought, such as I fail at everything I do, gets repeated, it becomes sticky, and you may live it out. After a breakup, you may think, See, I'm a total failure even at love. In this case, the cognitive distortion "all-or-nothing thinking" has trapped you, making you believe it. Harder to ignore now, this distorted thought can lead you to feeling depressed or anxious.

The practice of naming, not shaming, what you're experiencing (I'm having anxious thoughts, or I feel depressed) can help you shift toward an attitude of acceptance—not because you enjoy thinking or feeling this way but because this attitude will help you heal. *How?*, you may be asking. As you accept your reality instead of fighting it, you can then put more of your energy toward your breakup recovery. In essence, the naming lets you pause, even if just for a few seconds, so you can rethink before you react. You get to reframe your thinking to be more accepting. See, I'm a total failure even at love becomes Yes, I made mistakes, and I can learn from them. This self-compassionate view will help you gain so much more than what you lost. Improving your self-esteem and knowing what feels right for you in your relationships is the goal.

Congratulations on reaching the third and final section of this book: *Shine.* So far, you've faced the pain of your breakup and you've begun the healing process. These remaining chapters aim to help your comeback as you let go of the emotional attachment to your ex. Your comeback is fluid, gradual, and without a deadline. It occurs as you continue to rediscover yourself. Your interest in activities will increase, meaning and purpose will return, and thoughts of your loss will no longer consume your time. You'll make new connections. You'll either be thinking about starting to date again or may even be dating. Your thoughts about your future will be optimistic.

As we continue on the journey of your comeback, I want to first share the metaphor of a broken vase. It has been said that adversity—the tough times or painful events a person endures—leads them to view their world or themselves as shattered, like a broken vase. Some people will try to put their lives back together exactly as before. But like a vase glued back together, their lives remain fractured and vulnerable. However, those who accept the breakage and build themselves up from a refreshed perspective become resilient, strong, and open to new things (Joseph 2013).

So, like a broken vase that gets built anew, let's do this for you. Let's build you up from within, starting at your inner core, where it all begins.

Get to the Core of It

What causes us to believe our half-truths or think so badly about ourselves when we're hurting the most? The answer can be found in understanding the root cause of our critical voice. Automatic negative thoughts on repeat are pervasive; they occur in all different scenarios and often without warning or justification. Chances are that these thoughts are the externalization (self-talk) of what we experience internally based on our deep-rooted core beliefs. *Core beliefs* are the way we view ourselves, others, and the world, and they can be either positive or negative. Those that are negative can be problematic and lasting.

Let's dig in to better understand core beliefs about the self so you can recognize your own and see how they shape your decision making and personality.

- They are often developed early in life, by our childhood experiences.

- They significantly shape our reality and behaviors.

- They may be subconscious beliefs that we are not even aware of.

- They get exaggerated by our underlying assumptions, the negative judgments we make about ourselves.

- They often fall into three categories (Beck 2005):

    - Helplessness (believing oneself to be incompetent, vulnerable, or with inferior abilities),

    - Worthlessness (believing oneself to be insignificant, a burden to others, or worthless), or

    - Unlovability (believing oneself to be incapable of obtaining the desired attention and intimacy).

Break Free from Your Past Hurts

If it is flooded every day with negative core beliefs (such as I'm a total mess), your brain will keep processing new information through this lens. Remember, core beliefs can be in your subconscious, so you may not even notice them. Instead, you may make assumptions or exaggerated judgments of your present experiences (People tend to leave me) that reinforce the faulty self-beliefs. Left unchallenged, unhealthy breakup traps (I will always be alone) are unfortunately strengthened.

In the context of a breakup, let's look at what happens when a core belief pairs with a negative assumption, reinforcing the breakup thinking trap your brain has automatically gone to.

I'm stuck (core belief of helplessness). Nothing I do helps me feel better (negative assumption). I'll never get over this breakup (catastrophizing).

It's all my fault (core belief of helplessness). Even when I try, I fail (negative assumption). I can't do anything right (all-or-nothing thinking).

I'm invisible (core belief of worthlessness). No one ever notices me (negative assumption). I'm not enough (personalizing).

I'm a disaster (core belief of worthlessness). I mess everything up (negative assumption). I'll ruin every relationship I ever have (fortune telling).

I'm unlikeable (core belief of unlovability). No one likes me (negative assumption). I'll be alone forever (catastrophizing).

I'm a loser (core belief of unlovability). Everyone eventually leaves me (negative assumption). I'll never find love (overgeneralizing).

If you notice any similarities or patterns in your own self-statements, write about them in your journal.

As you can see, core beliefs are maintained by the underlying assumptions or rules we create from our past experiences. If left unchallenged, these faulty assumptions stored in our brains will activate our critical voice and misguide our behaviors or actions. That's why we need to question these assumptions instead of taking them as absolutes or full truths. Pausing to question self-beliefs can help keep them from getting even more ingrained and permanent. That way, moving forward, you'll examine your beliefs based on their merit (Does this thought serve me? or Is there a better way to think about this?) instead of habit. You'll examine the origin of your negative self-talk (What causes me to think this way? or Why do I feel that I'm not enough?). Here's how it works:

- On autorepeat, the negative thought I pushed my ex away can lead you to feel bad about yourself and even make you feel anxious or depressed.

- By connecting past or recent hurts to how you react or think in the present, you'll gain valuable information about yourself. I never felt like a priority in my relationship.

- Your compassionate voice here encourages a nonjudgmental view of yourself. My constant need for reassurance from my ex makes sense to me.

- By challenging your self-talk, you gain a broader view of your situation. You'll pivot toward helpful insights. This insight helps me understand why I reacted the way I did.

Uncover What Is Fueling You

Are you starting to see how healing from a breakup truly starts in your mind? How you choose to think about yourself is what moves you toward self-love and an improved connection to others. It's commonly said that a person is flooded with approximately sixty thousand thoughts per day, ranging from simple daily tasks to deep contemplations about life and the world in which we live (Luskin and Pelletier 2005). Since thoughts are repetitive and formed from your core beliefs, it's important to challenge the ones that cause harm. How do you do that? By bringing subconscious beliefs into consciousness, allowing you to see when there is a mismatch between your thoughts and their effects.

You can use the downward arrow technique to help uncover the more upsetting beliefs so that they're easier to notice and not act on (Gillihan 2018). The name of this technique comes from the downward arrows used to trace the line of thinking, which is shown in the next exercise. You can write your own answers in your journal so you can see how this process can help:

- Write down one negative thought about your breakup that has been bothering you.

- Be curious. Ask yourself, What does this mean about me?

- Keep going until you get to your underlying core beliefs, listening for the common themes of helplessness, worthlessness, and unlovability.

Thought: I can't believe my friends aren't asking me how I'm doing. My breakup was only a month ago!

↓

What does this mean about me? It means they don't understand me.

↓

What does this mean about me? It means they don't care about me.

↓

What does this mean about me? It means no one cares about me.

↓

What does this mean about me? It means that there is something wrong with me because no one cares about me.

↓

Core belief: I'm not worthy of being cared about by others.

Dig deep. The question What does this mean about me? can help uncover your assumptions or judgments about yourself. Notice that with each downward arrow, you get to a more distressing thought. Now it's easier to understand feeling ashamed or depressed. If you need some extra help to get to your core belief, add these other questions:

- What am I worried about?

- What do I think will happen?

- How might I handle that if it does happen?

- Why does that matter if that happens?

- Where does this thought come from?

- Is there another explanation or possible outcome?

This approach breaks down what is most upsetting for you so you can tolerate it better. Hearing what's going on for you can help reduce depression. Looking back at my breakup story, I wish I had known this. I was seeking reassurance from others to feel better. I needed to better understand how my core belief of unlovability (I'm not enough) was fueling my thinking in extremes (I will never find love) and resulted in my feeling both anxious and depressed.

This process of challenging negative core beliefs isn't about turning every negative into a positive. You don't want to ignore what is coming to your surface. Instead, focus on hearing from your inner wounds so you can move toward healing them. Self-love comes from this awareness:

I'm realizing what my core beliefs sound like, and this is a step toward healing.

I went through something painful, and it has affected me.

Knowing my core beliefs can help me begin to challenge their accuracy.

This can help me act in ways that better reflect what I have learned from my experiences.

Inhale, pause, exhale. As the painful self-beliefs surface, practice combining mindful breathing and your pause button to sit with the discomfort. Use the Triangle of Change (TOC) below as your guide. As you move through the steps of naming what you're feeling or thinking, count out your inhales and exhales. Plant your feet firmly, square your shoulders comfortably, and compassionately accept your thoughts. You're tolerating your discomfort, not trying to fix it or avoid it. Practice it:

Name it: I'm realizing that I have thoughts of worthlessness.

Inhale—1...2...3.

Pause to let in the self-love: It makes sense to me.

Exhale—1...2...3.

Tame it: I can learn from this.

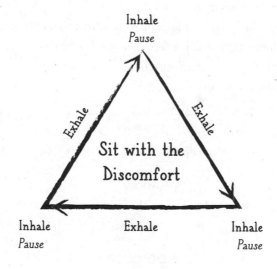

Inhale
Pause

Exhale   Exhale

Sit with the
Discomfort

Inhale   Exhale   Inhale
Pause   Pause

Tolerate discomfort. Learning to sit with your emotions gives you the freedom to find your steady, balanced, and solid footing, to just be with your unpleasant thoughts and feelings. You learn to accept that you don't need to do anything specific. There is no need for you to act on your thoughts and urges, and there is no long-term benefit to avoiding them either. Just breathe, pause, and observe your balanced and steady footing as it's forming. When practicing the above TOC (inhale, pause, exhale), simply be present with whatever you are experiencing in the moment.

Let's look at an example of how to use this technique:

You finally agree to go out with your friends this Friday night instead of staying home and overthinking your relationship. You're nervous, as you haven't seen your friends outside of school in a while. You're considering canceling. You name what you're experiencing (I'm having anxiety about going to the football game). You accept it as is. You allow yourself to sit with this discomfort (This makes sense to me. I just reconnected with this friend group. I'm sure it will be fine once we get caught up.).

I encourage you to add an **approach** step to this accept-and-allow technique. This additional step will encourage you to make choices and practice healthy behaviors to jump-start your change process.

Let's break this down even more:

Accept
I'm having anxiety about going to the football game.

Allow
This makes sense to me. I just reconnected
with this friend group.

Approach
I'm sure it will be fine after we spend some time
getting caught up. I believe that I can deal with this.

The next TOC is a good visual reminder and grounding exercise to get you moving toward your healthier mindset and steady footing.

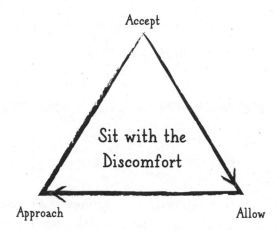

As you practice this TOC, you may feel uncomfortable at first. The goal here is not to make you happy about your unpleasant thoughts but rather to help you become less affected by them. A lot has changed because of your breakup, and a lot may be surfacing for you. As you become more comfortable with the uncomfortable, you'll move toward thinking about other more helpful things. Your thoughts will become more flexible, moving from I won't ever get over this to I'm struggling to get over this. I hope these shifts are beginning to ignite your self-love.

Try it. The next time you have the thought to check your ex's social media, pause and listen for a possible faulty assumption. This may sound like I have to know what they're doing tonight before I do anything else or I should check on them after causing all this pain. Instead, pivot toward a more secure narrative:

I have an urge to check their socials, and it's okay.

Just because I'm thinking about calling them doesn't mean I have to.

I'm still not used to being single.

I'm learning ways to sit with these uncomfortable feelings.

There are other things I can do instead; I can call a friend, listen to music, or journal my feelings.

I'm shifting my focus to things that are in my best interests.

Let's Recap

It's completely normal to push away or avoid unpleasant feelings, especially when breakup pain feels so intense and uncomfortable. The problem is, this approach works for only a while and can make you feel worse, not better, in the long run. Over time, resisting intense thoughts or avoiding them will make them stickier, more difficult to ignore, and longer lasting. Learning to tolerate, not avoid, your unpleasant and difficult intense emotions (rejection, rage, depression, anxiety, guilt) is how you confront these unpleasant thoughts and feelings. By sitting with these intense emotions, you're not giving in to them or avoiding them. You are changing your attitude toward these thoughts—and as your thoughts become less intense, they will have less impact on you.

For a fulfilling and meaningful life, I encourage you to be open to all your inner experiences as they occur, especially the unpleasant and gut-wrenching ones. Remember, as you reclaim your secure ground, with the balance and steady footing that come from self-acceptance, you're gaining the skills to be present so you can break free from your thinking traps.

Hear Your Compassionate Voice

As you continue down your path of rediscovery, you'll find opportunities for decision making, growth, and healing. Meeting these moments with a steady footing is what you and I have been working toward by nurturing your self-acceptance, hope, and skills. Being in the know, asking curious questions, and countering unhealthy urges and thinking traps have paved the way. Keep practicing these coping skills to improve your self-esteem by pivoting away from a negative self-view and toward one that keeps your best interests in mind.

To move on from your ex, reflecting on how you relate or *attach* (connect emotionally) in romantic relationships can highlight which patterns hinder your having the healthy relationship you desire. Use a curious and straightforward mindset to uncover how you attach:

- What originally attracted me to my ex?

- Did I feel comfortable sharing my innermost thoughts and feelings with my ex?

- When we argued, did I yell and scream? Did I shut down and avoid conflict?

- Did my anxiety or depression impact the relationship?

- Did my vulnerabilities drive my reactions?

- Was I unhappy with the relationship more often than I was happy?

- Was I aware when my partner needed kindness?

Knowing which category of core beliefs (worthlessness, helplessness, or unlovability) gets kicked up in your relationships is useful. Remember, core beliefs can be either positive or negative. If you believe I'm worthwhile, competent, and lovable, you'll likely have more positive views about your relationships and make decisions with self-confidence. In contrast, negative self-beliefs will likely have a troublesome impact on your personality and decision making.

Going back to my breakup story, the core belief I'm not enough led to my feeling both insecure and anxious when we were apart while dating. As a result, I craved excessive reassurance that things were fine between us, which made my anxiety worse in the long run and led to my relationship rumination. As we'll explore, an insecure attachment style can negatively affect both relationship quality and breakup suffering for one or both partners. Let this truth empower your nonjudgmental and healing journey.

Your Brain Got Attached to Your Ex Too

According to *attachment theory*, each of us has an attachment mechanism in our brains that develops in infancy and seeks to establish a sense of security between ourselves and our parent or primary caregiver (Bowlby 1980). Our early interactions with these adults serve to demonstrate the dependability or lack thereof in our relationships. This mechanism is still at work in adulthood, when we seek emotionally supportive social and romantic relationships.

Basically, the messages that our brains receive about whether we can depend on loving and attentive responses from another are what form and maintain our emotional balance. When parents are responsive to the needs of their baby, the child learns that the parent is available and attentive, and a secure attachment is formed. Securely attached children grow up better able to regulate their emotions and are generally able to attach in healthy ways in romantic relationships. They will lean toward closeness, trusting that they will receive care and comfort when needed. Alternatively, when parents are distant or inconsistent with their caregiving, the child will adapt by avoiding them— for example, by focusing on their toys rather than approaching the caregiver—in order to feel safe and to regulate their intense emotions. Insecure attachments are formed when a relationship has elements of mistrust, does not feel safe, and lacks a secure base. Insecure attachments can be either *anxious* or *avoidant* in nature. An avoidant person struggles with or feels anxiety or sadness, but does so alone.

Understanding your attachment style can help you name the relationship triggers or core beliefs that come up for you and how these affect your personality and actions. Consider these questions: Did your ex ever complain that you were smothering or suffocating them? Then you might have anxious attachment. Did you stay away on purpose to keep yourself from getting too attached? Then you might have avoidant attachment.

As you consider your own attachment style, it can be helpful to understand the personality of your ex and how their behaviors made you feel. Would your ex get mad at you if they were unable to reach you? Perhaps they have anxious attachment. Did you often feel deprived or ignored while dating your ex? Then they might have avoidant attachment. It's also possible to have traits from both categories of insecure attachment, anxious and avoidant.

The exercise that follows gives a brief overview of the three different types of attachment: anxious, avoidant, or secure. I touch upon this topic here to help you connect your inner beliefs to how you relate to other people. There are many books fully dedicated to attachment style, and I encourage you to read more if the topic interests you. For now, let's get a foundation to show you how the different attachment styles may play out in your relationships.

In your journal, write down the statements that most resonate with you, or download the list and put a check next to those statements. Count your responses in each list to determine which attachment style may apply to you. You can also read through the lists a second time to see whether any particular one describes your ex's personality and behaviors.

Your attachment style is **anxious** if you relate to the following:

- I count the hours it takes for the person I like to respond to my Snaps/texts/calls.

- I disclose too much information when I first start dating someone.

- I constantly think about, fantasize, or obsess over my partner.

- I can be clingy and then get angry when my needs are not met.

- I struggle with jealousy.

- I often feel incomplete without my partner.

- I seek frequent reassurance from my partner.

- My mood and self-worth are based on my partner's validation.

- I am sensitive to criticism.

- I fear abandonment, rejection, and conflict.

Your attachment style is **avoidant** if you relate to the following:

- I worry about losing my freedom and independence.

- I come across as disinterested or distant.

- I often find flaws in my partners soon after we start dating.

- I often spend time away from my partner.

- I find it difficult to ask others for help.

- I don't like to talk about my feelings.

- I have difficulty expressing my needs and wants.

- I chase people with whom I have an incompatible future.

- I will withdraw if a relationship seems to be getting too serious.

- I am uncomfortable with conflict.

Your attachment style is **secure** if you relate to the following:

- I define my self-esteem and identity on my own, without needing my partner's reinforcement.

- I am comfortable with emotional intimacy.

- I can express my boundaries freely.

- I respect my partner's privacy and boundaries.

- I can communicate my feelings and needs in my relationships.

- I tend to be attentive and loving.

- I trust my partner and their feelings for me.

- I am committed to my partner, yet independent.

- I can self-soothe when upset and restore my emotional balance.

- I can communicate during conflict and work through the problem.

I hope this exercise gave you some things to think about regarding both you and those you're attracted to. In general, the securely attached know their worth, can give and receive support comfortably, and are steady in the face of adversity. The anxiously attached tend to be overly dependent on their partner. They crave intimacy, doubt their worth, and seek reassurance. The avoidant seeks to be independent and will refrain from getting too intimate with another. They will feel suffocated, see love as work, and may even sabotage close relationships.

Let's say you see yourself having a tendency toward insecurely attaching to another insecurely attached person. The attraction between anxious people and avoidants is common and usually stems from each having unconscious desires to satisfy unmet emotional needs from the past. The anxiously attached, familiar with being denied emotional closeness, will pursue connection and reassurance from their partner. When they finally receive the attention they desire, they feel reassured, valued. The avoidantly attached learn early on to be independent, as their primary caregiver was often unavailable and discouraged crying and emotional expression. An avoidant, aware of their issues with intimacy, will be attracted to their anxious pursuer, who represents the closeness they have missed out on.

Put these two attachment styles together, and what results is neither partner getting their emotional needs met. All the pursuing and distancing behaviors can be thought of as a manic push-pull or a whole lot of chaos that causes confusion. The extreme emotional highs and lows of the relationship are mistaken for passion, and the feelings of insecurity are familiar and mistaken for safety (Chan 2020).

Becoming More Secure in Relationships

Simply put, the anxiously attached fear abandonment and the avoidants fear rejection. In contrast, people who are securely attached inherently feel safe in their relationships. They appreciate their own self-worth and trust their ability to meet their own needs. They are comfortable being themselves in their relationships and can rely on others in times of adversity.

According to the research, we all have the basic brain wiring to be in a relationship that is

grounded in feeling secure (We protect each other),

collaborative (We're in this together),

fair (We quickly repair any hurts that occur),

mutual (What's good for one of us is good for both), and

sensitive (We're aware of each other's needs) (Tatkin 2016).

Sometimes we need to strengthen that wiring to offset what has been previously established. Remember the brain train? Let's say that the old track—the neural pathway—of disconnection has become familiar and automatic. The pause-and-pivot can help here to move the brain train away from the insecure track and toward the steady and more secure track.

The following Triangle of Change can demonstrate this lesson. This time, a downward arrow is used on both sides of the triangle. Trace your finger along the side you feel most represents you. As you move toward steady footing, visualize yourself becoming more secure in your attachments and learning how to stop unhealthy intimacy patterns in their tracks.

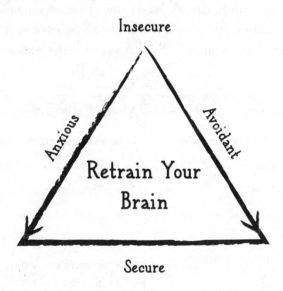

To become more secure, the track (neural connections) that leads to healthy connections needs to be strengthened. For the anxiously attached, the work is to help yourself feel safe instead of needing someone else to do it for you. Try this: the next time you're waiting for someone to respond to your text, practice self-soothing (do some mindful breathing or wash your face). This can help you resist the urges and tolerate the discomfort, knowing that the intensity will eventually subside if you give it time and space.

An avoidant will feel the symptoms of their distress (increased heart rate, stress, rage, and so on) yet struggle getting to the root of their feelings. To become more secure, avoidants should engage in meaningful conversations around difficult feelings with their partner. Sharing during a conflict instead of running away is a good place to start.

Understanding why you attach the way you do can be very grounding as you make new connections. To help, let's consider the emotions that fuel the neural pathway toward disconnection, where your behavior is needy and clingy, or selfish and stand-offish. Plus, as you continue to move through this breakup stage—your comeback—it's a good reminder to hear what your emotions are telling you. Let's look at another breakdown to better understand insecure attachments:

Anxious Attachment	Avoidant Attachment
What is my anxiety telling me?	What is my avoidance telling me?
• I'm invisible. • I'm all alone. • I can't focus on anything else. • I have lost everything. • I don't matter. • This is the worst thing possible. • No one loves me. • I will always suffer like this.	• I can't trust anyone. • I'm better off alone. • I feel so overwhelmed. • My emotions don't matter. • I don't know how to be direct. • I'm a total mess. • Nothing ever works out for me. • I'm not good at relationships.

Anxious Attachment	Avoidant Attachment
To become more secure:	To become more secure:
• I can recognize that I'm having anxiety.	• I can recognize that these are learned assumptions.
• I can resist the urge to seek reassurance.	• I will talk about my feelings to someone I trust.
• I can focus on small things I can do instead that will bring me some joy.	• I will not jump to conclusions about my future relationships.
• I will tell myself that I'm worthy of love on my own merits.	• I will focus on learning about myself and understanding, without judgment, why I react this way.
• I can remind myself that I'm not alone.	• I will remind myself that avoiding things will make me feel worse in the long run.
• I can do something opposite.	• I will focus on the things that I like about myself.
• I can make plans to meet up with a friend.	• I will see that relationships can be fulfilling.
• I can practice self-compassion and treat myself with kindness and care like I would a friend going through something similar.	

Hopefully this exercise has shown that you have choices that can help you make improvements for yourself. As you do more things that are proactive, or good for you, you're strengthening the neural pathway to feeling secure. Let's look at how Charlotte is working through her recent relationship.

• Charlotte's Story

Since her breakup with Josh three months ago, Charlotte has been going to therapy on a weekly basis. She told her therapist that Josh would call her too needy during their arguments and that he couldn't handle all her emotions. They would spend more time arguing about his needing space from her than dealing with any of their problems. This made Charlotte feel that her feelings didn't matter.

Early in therapy, Charlotte would spend a lot of time complaining about Josh and how angry she was at him. During one session, Charlotte got so upset that she wanted to call Josh right then and there to tell him how he had messed her up forever. At first, her therapist encouraged Charlotte to consider what her anger was telling her, and then they processed what the consequences would be for her if she called Josh while she was so angry.

Charlotte's therapist is helping her recognize that she is using her *reacting brain*, with its impulsive choices and likely negative consequences. Encouraging Charlotte to listen nonjudgmentally to what her emotions are telling her starts the process of her finding ways to work through them. This process will move her toward her *thinking brain*, the more rational and intentional response system. Being intentional means Charlotte will consider what is in her best interests so she can make a conscious choice. This will help Charlotte find her steady footing so she can best manage herself.

The following TOC can help you practice the grounding experience of going from being charged up to being intentional (thinking instead of reacting). Looking at this TOC, notice that you are encouraged to trace your finger down either side to experience the downward flow of energy as you move toward finding your more secure attachment style. Let your curious voice guide you to think things through in a conscious and steady way: How might things be different for me as I feel more safe, stable, and satisfied in my close relationships?

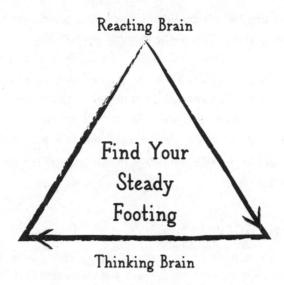

Reacting Brain

Find Your
Steady
Footing

Thinking Brain

Consider also how becoming more secure and calm can improve your communication and conflict resolution skills. Dialectical behavioral therapy (DBT) encourages being mindful and using self-soothing skills to calm down before attempting to settle a conflict. This way, you stay grounded in your values, listen, and validate the other person. You can assert yourself in a clear, concise, and matter-of-fact manner. If the conflict remains unresolved or the conversation is unproductive, revisit the conflict later (Pederson 2017). This approach can increase your sense of self-respect and your ability to build and take care of your relationships.

Sharing your needs either before or during an argument (This is a hard discussion for me) is one example of how to use this approach. Or you could stop mid-argument to let the other person know that you hear their message or to ask for clarification to make sure you two are on the same page. This can sound like "What I'm hearing you say is…" or "Can you clarify that last point for me?" Think about the last time you said to someone "I agree with you" or "I hear you." Or try saying this the next time you're in an argument. Watch how it can change the mood and direction of the conversation.

By using a calm and compassionate voice, your self-esteem will be thankful. You are giving yourself an in-the-moment opportunity to say, I'm getting better at managing conflicts. Self-compassion is defined as the process by which we turn compassion inward. It's supporting and encouraging ourselves, instead of being overly harsh and judgmental, when challenges and difficulties arise (Neff 2011). Basically, you speak to yourself how you would to a friend who is going through something similar. Let's look at how Logan is struggling with his breakup. His story gives a review of several lessons learned, including self-compassion.

• Logan's Story

It's been over three months since Logan's boyfriend, Sean, broke up with him at the beginning of the fall semester, saying that he needed to focus on school. Logan was a junior and Sean was a sophomore, and they both went to the same college. Shocked, Logan immediately shut down, and he spent the next few weeks mostly by himself in his dorm room. He rarely went to his classes or responded to his friends' calls or texts.

Logan was convinced there was another reason Sean broke up with him. He spent most days replaying memories in his head of their relationship, and he still couldn't figure out what happened. Logan was finding random things to blame himself for the breakup: Maybe I should have gone to more of his band rehearsals? *and* I should have been more supportive. *He kept second-guessing himself, and he felt like he was going crazy.*

As the shock of their breakup began to wear off, Logan started to go back to the gym on campus, and he resumed some of his other usual activities. Soon after, Logan saw Sean near the student center, laughing with some friends Logan didn't recognize. Feeling his heart start to race, Logan decided to approach Sean. They were each civil to the other at first. When Sean said he was going to be late for class, Logan started questioning him relentlessly about their breakup. Not getting any specific reason from Sean, Logan felt dismissed and out of control. He cursed and screamed at Sean and pushed him out of his way.

Sean's friends quickly escorted him away. Crying and ashamed of himself, Logan ran back to his dorm, and he started texting Sean feverishly to apologize.

What breakup recovery roadblocks did Logan experience in this scenario?

- He isolated himself and therefore didn't receive the support or empathy from his network that he rightfully deserved.

- He spent his time ruminating over his breakup and relationship, which didn't give him any new information and only made him feel worse.

- Seeing Sean on campus unexpectedly affected his emotions. He experienced a fight-flight-or-freeze response.

- His isolation kicked up feelings of worthlessness and unlovability.

- His uncontrolled anger caused him to do and say things that he regretted afterward.

- All of the above.

If you answered "All of the above," you're correct. If Logan were your friend, I bet you'd be thinking of many things to say to him to help him feel better. You might even share this book with Logan, telling him it's a worthy read (lol). You likely would validate his feelings (It's okay to not be okay) and add that while no two breakups are the same, you relate to what he is going through. You might even praise his sharing with you how he's doing, knowing that isolating ourselves when we are going through something difficult is never a good idea.

You could encourage Logan to think beyond figuring out why Sean called it quits and focus more on his own mental health recovery. He could do activities that bring him joy or get him back on track with his classes. You might suggest that Logan accept that he may never know the real reason for their relationship ending, and that focusing on what he learned is more in his best interests.

The hope is that Logan would use your helpful insights to find the balance he was seeking. He would find validation in his compassionate voice. His outward reactions to seeing Sean arose because he was hurting and fighting to get answers. He would acknowledge that by isolating, he denied himself the support he deserved and was being offered. He would agree to reach out for help or make plans to see a friend or do something that he enjoys if he feels bad again.

Let's Recap

Listening to your emotions can give you a better sense of how you react to stress and how you relate to others. These insights can help you pivot toward healing as you continue your comeback. Your sense of self-respect and acceptance, and your care for yourself and your relationships, are things you can continue to nurture. As you make plans and new connections, you can speak to what you need and what is in your best interests.

An example: Say you have been feeling alone lately as your friend group changed after your breakup. Try thinking about a friend you have something in common with or who may be more likely to return your text. You could try texting I know it's been a while since we talked, but I wanted to say hi and catch up. Even if you don't hear back, the effort you made to change your connections is a step toward feeling more secure and finding your steady footing.

SKILL 9

Rebuild with Confidence

Navigating your breakup has undoubtedly not been easy. It's likely been grueling, complicated, and even scary at times. Every part of your day-to-day life and functioning were affected. You lost everything you once knew to be yours and counted on: your special person, your routine, your identity. Whether you were in a long-term relationship or had gone on only a few dates, you also lost the hope of a future together. The thrill and security that come from being a couple were shattered too. Whether you initiated the breakup or not, you likely doubted yourself and your expectations. Hopefully, you've found your solid footing as you've weathered the emotional roller coaster during the stages of your breakup: protest (crying, anger, yearning), disorganization (negative self-talk, anxiety, depression), and recovery (acceptance, finding meaning, having a new plan in place).

As you rebuild your life, listen for your refreshed narrative and feel empowered by all you've gained. Improved understanding of what makes you happy and balanced is here. Moving forward on your continued healing journey, remember that you have choices: how you think about yourself, who you spend time with, and what you need to feel emotionally secure. Perhaps the pain from wondering Who am I without them? has pivoted toward healing: I've gained truly helpful insights about myself. You asked the painful questions early on because you were seeking ways to move through the intense pain to regain your steady and calm self.

The coping skill of being curious has been used throughout this book to encourage your own emerging self-awareness of what you need and can do for yourself to feel better. Truly, the answers to living confidently and emotionally connected to others are within your own story of pain and recovery. Look back to any prior relationships, romantic or with your parents or caregivers, for insights and compassion for yourself and them too. Remember, attachment style affects all of us differently, as do faulty core beliefs that can be long lasting and misleading. Once you better understand your reasons for how you relate to others (I always felt left out as a kid), be mindful of pivoting your curiosity toward your present self (How can I think more confidently here?).

To stay on this constructive path of healing, remember that your brain—your neural and attachment systems—are affected by your breakup too. This is why you may crave seeing your ex again or knowing what they're up to. Checking your ex's social media, even if only occasionally, is like when an ex-smoker takes a drag of a cigarette, or an alcoholic who has been sober for a while has a drink again, making it harder to resist the urge the next time and threatening the newly found healthful path. A person can become addicted to love as much as they can to a drug or alcohol.

Romantic love triggers the release of dopamine, a neurotransmitter that helps produce the euphoria you feel when you think of your ex, or when someone seeks another drug fix or drink. As feelings get evoked, positive or negative, your brain will keep you craving more to balance itself. Whether you're face to face, online, or reliving memories through old photos or posts, any unresolved issues will surface too. Choosing to do this when you're stressed may seem necessary, yet in the long run it will make you feel worse. The skill is to practice sitting with the discomfort of wanting to contact your ex, knowing that as you wait it out, the urge to do so will dissipate. Better for you to be curious: What can I do right now that is in my best interests?

Your Relationship Bucket

Here's a visual exercise to practice if you can't stop thinking about your ex or you're considering whether to get back together. Picture a bucket that is large enough to hold the memories of your relationship. A filled bucket would represent when you feel connected to your partner—securely attached, understood, respected. The bucket may have some holes in it, which represent times you grew apart or when one of you was distant, in effect, lowering your level of relationship satisfaction since what you once relied upon has seeped out of the holes.

Looking back at your relationship, did either or both of you try to patch up the holes? If so, did your bucket get refilled? Perhaps your relationship got stronger, even overflowing with meaningful connection. Or did the holes get bigger and harder to repair? This image can tell you a lot about how much you and your partner were willing and able to do to mend the holes in your relationship, and whether the holes can even be fixed.

Remember too whether your relationship bucket ever got kicked over entirely, dumping out everything from your time together or causing the breakup. Did one of you cheat with someone else? Was there any sexting to anyone outside your relationship that was later discovered? Or did your partner force you to send explicit pictures to them? Were there lies or secrets related to drugs, porn use, finances, or anything else, that were later discovered? These lies and secrets are *relationship norm violations* (RNVs) that fracture a relationship and lead to mistrust, guilt, and shame. Beyond the betrayal that these behaviors cause, the concern is their impact on your self-esteem, overall mental health, body image, and safety.

According to the research, when a fracture occurs in a relationship, it can be one partner's way of either making or breaking the relationship. Even sexting with someone outside the relationship can be considered cheating (Nelson 2012). Whether intended to bring life back to a dull relationship or to ensure its finality, recognize what the fracture and the feelings along with it are telling you. RNVs can teach you which holes in your relationship bucket can be patched, and which ones are beyond repair. Walking away is the big step toward recovering your sense of self: what you need, expect, and offer to keep any relationship bucket you share with someone healthy, rock solid, and overflowing. It's in these types of relationships where you'll shine bright, and get to live and love your best life.

Rewrite Your Own Acceptance Letter

Ever wonder why you keep repeating the same patterns of relating to others, even if those ways are not in your best interests? Do you try to be something that you're not just to get your crush to notice you? Or does it seem that you keep being attracted to people who aren't available? Instead of I have to convince her to like me, try a steadier thought: I think the two of us might have some things in common. This reframed thought can help you think through next steps: I'll ask her to go to the movies this weekend. Even if she says no, I'll be glad that I tried.

For me, validating my own worth and uniqueness was what helped me realize that the holes in our relationship bucket were irreparable. I decided to pay less attention to the kind of environments that stressed me out and instead to focus on all the little things that brought me life. It was then that I decided to rewrite my own acceptance letter, mapping out how I would speak to myself during difficult times and the things I would and would not accept from others.

So how do you confidently move forward? We've been working toward you gaining a self-appraisal that is accepting (Where do I get stuck?), wise (What is in my best interests?), and self-soothing (What will help me feel better?). Next, let's help you come up with your own unique definition of relationship satisfaction for the next part of your life. Figuring out ways to effectively manage intense emotions, which are unavoidable in life, and how you want to engage in your relationships are both important and very much within your control. Your values and boundaries contribute to you moving forward in a constructive way with your solid footing.

Knowing how you want your relationships, both romantic and otherwise, to look and sound can help you pay attention to what you value in others. Do you know people who energize you instead of draining you? Are there people in your life you look forward to seeing? Paying attention to all the ways you can spend more time around people and doing things that bring you joy can support your healing journey. Feeling secure or emotionally safe in this way is when you feel supported, understood, and with a sense of belonging. While feeling less stress is appealing, try not to minimize the positive impact from your high-stakes relationships, like your parents, teachers, or boss. Beyond their expectations of you, they too can be wonderful sources of support. After all, they want you to continue growing and learning.

What you need to feel secure in a relationship is important to consider as you heal and move on. Perhaps there were parts of your relationship with your ex that you knew weren't in your best interests. Consider how your communication and conflict resolution style may have hindered your happiness in your relationship. Some things to consider:

- How would you describe your fighting style?

- Do you argue the same way with your parents as you would with a romantic partner?

- Do you know the difference between a good fight and a bad one?

- If you could improve how you fight, what would you change?

- Do you apologize and then work on making changes to help yourself and your partner feel better?

- Do you apologize to your partner to make the argument stop?

- Do you try to repair things after a fight, or do you prefer to forget and move on?

Let's break this down even further. Not all red flags mean that a relationship is doomed, but recognizing the red flags can help you know what to look out for as non-negotiables, or can help them be addressed before they get ingrained in your relationship. Green flags are relationship characteristics that you have either experienced already or want to have that make you feel safe and secure in a relationship. This list isn't exhaustive by any means. Green flags, as well as red flags, are very personal. For example, dating someone who is habitually late may be a red flag for you, but your best friend may have no problem with this behavior.

The chart that follows presents a list of common green and red flags in relationships. Download this chart and mark which traits are a "No way!" and which are a "Yes way!" You can also use your journal to write down those traits. Either way, you may want to jot down which traits remind you negatively and positively of your ex, to help you know what to look out for and what you prefer in your next romantic relationship.

Green Flags (Yes Way!)	Red Flags (No Way!)
My partner...	My partner...
accepts me for who I am.	is abusive and controlling.
appreciates my challenges and my strengths.	invades my privacy.
encourages my growth and learning.	avoids working on relationship problems.
listens to better understand me and what I need or don't like.	constantly interrupts me.
is open to feedback.	is jealous all the time.
can apologize and own up to their behavior.	is deceptive and lies.
tries to change.	takes me for granted.
shows me consistent caring behavior.	is quick to blame others.
gives me space and alone time when I need it or ask for it.	blames me for their behaviors.
	ignores my boundaries (what I need to feel safe and secure).
	has no interest in making any changes.

First Dates

The idea of dating again and putting yourself out there to possibly get hurt is daunting. So true, right? It takes time, patience, and figuring out your relationship expectations. Are you looking for a serious commitment or someone to spend some time with occasionally? What have you gained since your breakup that you're not willing to give up at this time? Perhaps you have enjoyed spending more time with your friends, or your grades have improved drastically since you eliminated the drama and chaos that was so common with your ex. You may wonder, How will I know I'm ready to start dating again?

Also, considering that you now know that rejection, guilt, and disappointment are some of the feelings associated with romantic relationships, how steady do you feel these days? Remember that the emotional, often painful, roller coaster of falling in love, dating, and breaking up is real. Yet you have learned a lot to help you regulate intense emotions, think through your choices, and find your balance. You have been there, done that. And now you have your emotional superpower, your pause button, to help you brake and know when to get off the roller coaster and onto steadier ground.

Think of your next talking stage or in-person date with someone new as practice. After all, you're either starting the conversation or keeping it going. Maintaining realistic expectations can reinforce your secure attachment to these experiences: I'm expecting that I will learn from this and that is what I'm seeking right now. If you do get disappointed, hurt, or rejected, the reminder that these experiences were trial runs can help. It makes sense, things don't always work out when meeting new people. That is how I'll learn what I'm looking for in my next romantic relationship.

Understanding your boundaries, where you end and the other person begins, can help you be more authentic and truer to your own needs when relating to others. Instead of being a people pleaser or putting the needs of others before your own, you'll make choices based on integrity and what makes the most sense for you. Boundary setting is a skill you can practice getting better at. It's when you choose to do something or not. When you set a boundary, you actively choose to feel discomfort in the present instead of second-guessing or feeling regret later. The next time someone asks you to do something that you'd rather not, try responding with "That doesn't work for me."

Trust that there is courage and strength in sharing. Be vulnerable, able to take a risk to show emotions or provide feedback despite fears or uncertainty of how it will be received. Listen to your truth and compassionate voice. Be authentic. Move away from I must go tonight or my friends will never ever ask me to dinner again and toward I don't feel up to it tonight, so I'll ask for a rain check.

In relationships, there are three boundary styles to consider: distant, enmeshed, and healthy. Each can occur in romantic relationships as well as with friends and family. As with any insight gained about ourselves, the idea is to better understand how we relate to others and what we feel we can improve upon to cultivate reciprocity and meaningful connections. While not an exhaustive list, the table that follows offers insights on these three types of boundaries.

In your journal, write out the statements that describe you and the people you're attracted to, whether romantically or not. Think about or write down ways you can move toward having healthier boundaries with others. Remember these prompts: What is in my best interest? What choices do I have?

A distant boundary means that you may...	An enmeshed boundary means that you may...	A healthy boundary means that you may...
avoid getting close	confuse where you end and they begin	communicate freely
find it hard to ask for help	always give in	say no and accept no from others
avoid sharing thoughts and feelings	overshare thoughts and feelings	voice your own values and opinions
shut down if things get too serious	need approval from others	put your needs over another's wants
leave without explanation (ghost)	get overinvolved with others	know when it's time to walk away

Relationship Breakthroughs

Research tells us that when we show ourselves kindness and compassion, our self-esteem increases (Neff 2011). *Self-compassion* is treating ourselves the same way we would a friend or loved one. Thinking about what makes us feel happy and balanced can move us forward in a hopeful and self-loving way. Perhaps since your breakup you joined a new club at school, started exercising again, or have raised your grades. Ask yourself:

What new things have I discovered about myself that I like?

What other parts of my life am I feeling good about?

When was the last time I felt I had a better day?

What was it about that day that made it better?

Maybe you haven't started anything new or made any obvious changes yet. That's okay. Today can be that day. In fact, to help with this, DBT encourages using the opposite action skill. To increase positive emotions, DBT suggests acting in ways opposite to the behaviors that are keeping you stuck in unwanted emotions. For example, if you find yourself procrastinating lately, pick one thing you have been putting off and do it today. Maybe it's reaching out to a friend, signing up for a cycle class, or wearing the adorable new jacket you bought when you went thrifting over a month ago. Or it could be as simple as getting up out of bed the first time your alarm goes off in the morning, instead of hitting the snooze button.

As you move toward your comeback, apply the opposite action skill to how you engage in your relationships. The notion here is that change occurs as you practice being flexible in your thinking and find the middle-ground options in your behaviors. For example, in a conflict, instead of keeping the argument going, pause and find something to agree with from the other person's point of view. Accept that any idea can have opposing truths, each with equal merit.

Let's look at another DBT skill called Both/And, which involves the space where two seemingly opposing truths are held at the same time. According to research, allowing both truths to coexist means you tolerate complexity in yourself and your relationships, thus creating resilience and healing (Solomon 2023).

Using this skill as you continue your comeback can validate your experiences and help you reinforce your solid footing. Basically, it's another way to train your brain to be more flexible with situations, accepting your realities instead of fighting them.

To practice this flexible mindset, repeat out loud the following statements that can help you appreciate the stabilizing nature of valid and opposing statements:

- I'm *both* weakened *and* empowered by my breakup.

- I feel *both* love *and* hate for my ex. .

- I'm *both* nervous *and* excited to be single again.

- I feel *both* dread *and* hope about starting over.

- I feel *both* supported *and* misunderstood by others.

- I feel *both* confused *and* prepared for next steps.

- I'm *both* disinterested *and* curious about dating in the digital age.

Your Comeback

I will leave you here with one last TOC that honors your journey toward rediscovery. Shall we go around this TOC together? Great! It will be my honor to do so, as it has been my honor to walk alongside you during our time here.

Rethink—Ask what your emotions are telling you right now.

Reset—Let your self-love be your guide toward steady footing.

Rebuild—Come back with confidence to a solid state of health, mind, and strength.

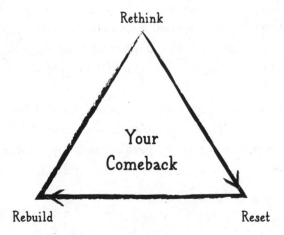

As you trace your finger around this TOC, experience the downward flow of energy as you securely breathe in and out, enjoying your calm and steady footing!

Let's Recap

Good for you! Here you are, having read through to the last chapter, making a new plan, and moving forward with balance and calm. I hope that you've already begun to live confidently and love compassionately. Let your self-awareness and compassion for yourself and others be your superpower. You can continue to learn about yourself and improve your self-esteem while connecting to others in a meaningful way.

Remember to use the TOCs that you learned in this book. These triangles are coping skills that you can use anytime you feel an intense emotion and want to shift your energy toward a calmer, steadier way of being. You can create your own TOC, or even trace your finger on any surface in the shape of a triangle, to practice your mindful breathing and benefit from this grounding exercise.

Remember, as well, that relationship issues and feeling intense emotions will happen. How you think about yourself, and your situation, will impact how strongly and how long you experience your emotions. Pausing and thinking through your next steps can help you spend less time stuck in unhelpful patterns and more time doing things in your best interest, which will make you feel better.

As you go about your days, I hope the lessons you've learned here continue to supercharge your self-love and make all your relationships, with family, friends, and romantic partners too, healthier and happier. Continue to take good care of *you*!

Acknowledgments

To the team at New Harbinger Publications, especially Georgia Kolias, Jennifer Holder, and Karen Schader: Thank you for believing in me and for the incredible guidance.

To all my family and friends: Thank you for all your love, support, and encouragement. You truly lifted me up when I needed it the most, and I'm forever grateful.

To my colleagues and mentors throughout my career: Your camaraderie and professionalism gave me something to believe in, and for that I commit to continuously improving and giving back to help the greater good.

Resources

To find a therapist:

www.psychologytoday.com

www.therapist.com

www.goodtherapy.org

If you're in crisis:

Call **911** or go to your nearest emergency room

Call **988** or visit www.988lifeline.org

References

Bowlby, J. 1980. *Attachment and Loss, Vol. 3: Loss*. New York: Basic Books.

Brown, B. 2017. *Braving the Wilderness: The Quest for True Belonging and the Courage to Stand Alone*. New York: Random House.

Chan, A. 2020. *Breakup Bootcamp: The Science of Rewiring Your Heart*. New York: HarperCollins.

Galanti, R. 2020. *Anxiety Relief for Teens: Essential CBT Skills and Mindfulness Practices to Overcome Anxiety and Stress*. New York: Random House.

Gillihan, S. 2018. *Cognitive Behavioral Therapy Made Simple: 10 Strategies for Managing Anxiety, Depression, Anger, Panic, and Worry*. New York: Althea Press.

Joseph, S. 2013. *What Doesn't Kill Us: The New Psychology of Posttraumatic Growth*. New York: Basic Books.

Luskin, F., and K. Pelletier. 2005. *Stress Free for Good: 10 Scientifically Proven Life Skills for Health and Happiness*. San Francisco, CA: HarperOne.

Mellody, P. 2003. *Facing Love Addiction: Giving Yourself the Power to Change the Way You Love*. San Francisco, CA: HarperOne.

Morin, A. 2014. *13 Things Mentally Strong People Don't Do: Take Back Your Power, Embrace Change, Face Your Fears, and Train Your Brain for Happiness and Success*. New York: HarperCollins.

Neff, K. 2011. *Self-Compassion: The Proven Power of Being Kind to Yourself*. New York: HarperCollins.

Nelson, T. 2012. *The New Monogamy: Redefining Your Relationship After Infidelity.* Oakland, CA: New Harbinger Publications.

Pederson, L. 2017. *The Expanded Dialectical Behavior Therapy Skills Training Manual: DBT for Self-Help, and Individual and Group Treatment Settings.* Eau Claire, WI: PESI.

Raja, S. 2021. *The Resilient Teen: 10 Key Skills to Bounce Back from Setbacks and Turn Stress into Success.* Oakland, CA: New Harbinger Publications.

Siegel, D. J., and T. P. Bryson. 2012. *The Whole-Brain Child: 12 Proven Strategies to Nurture Your Child's Developing Mind.* New York: Random House.

Solomon, A. 2023. *Love Every Day: 365 Relational Self-Awareness Practices to Help Your Relationship Heal, Grow, and Thrive.* Eau Claire, WI: PESI.

Tatkin, S. 2016. *Wired for Dating: How Understanding Neurobiology and Attachment Can Help You Find Your Ideal Mate.* Oakland, CA: New Harbinger Publications.

Van Dijk, S. 2021. *Don't Let Your Emotions Run Your Life for Teens: Dialectical Behavior Therapy Skills for Helping You Manage Mood Swings, Control Angry Outbursts, and Get Along with Others.* Oakland, CA: New Harbinger Publications.

Winch, G. 2018. *How to Fix a Broken Heart.* New York: TED Books/Simon & Schuster.

Winston, S., and M. Seif. 2017. *Overcoming Unwanted Intrusive Thoughts: A CBT-Based Guide to Getting Over Frightening, Obsessive, or Disturbing Thoughts.* Oakland, CA: New Harbinger Publications.

Lenora M. Ziegler, LCSW, is a licensed clinical social worker in private practice in Manalapan, NJ, where she specializes in working with teenagers, college students, and the adults who care for them. She is certified in anxiety treatment and dialectical behavior therapy (DBT), and it is her mission to help people improve their self-regulation, social media distress, and communication skills.

Real change *is* possible

For more than forty-five years, New Harbinger has published proven-effective self-help books and pioneering workbooks to help readers of all ages and backgrounds improve mental health and well-being, and achieve lasting personal growth. In addition, our spirituality books offer profound guidance for deepening awareness and cultivating healing, self-discovery, and fulfillment.

Founded by psychologist Matthew McKay and Patrick Fanning, New Harbinger is proud to be an independent, employee-owned company. Our books reflect our core values of integrity, innovation, commitment, sustainability, compassion, and trust. Written by leaders in the field and recommended by therapists worldwide, New Harbinger books are practical, accessible, and provide real tools for real change.

newharbingerpublications

More ⏱Instant Help Books for Teens

An Imprint of New Harbinger Publications

**THE GIRL'S GUIDE
TO RELATIONSHIPS,
SEXUALITY,
AND CONSENT**

Tools to Help Teens Stay Safe,
Empowered, and Confident

978-1684039739 / US $19.95

**THE TEEN GIRL'S
SURVIVAL JOURNAL**

Your Space to Learn, Reflect,
Explore, and Take Charge of
Your Mental Health

978-1648482861 / US $18.95

**THE ANGER
MANAGEMENT
WORKBOOK FOR
TEEN BOYS**

CBT Skills to Defuse Triggers,
Manage Difficult Emotions,
and Resolve Issues Peacefully

978-1684039074 / US $18.95

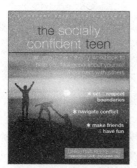

**THE SOCIALLY
CONFIDENT TEEN**

An Attachment Theory
Workbook to Help You Feel
Good about Yourself and
Connect with Others

978-1684038725 / US $18.95

**THE ANXIETY
AND DEPRESSION
WORKBOOK FOR TEENS**

Simple CBT Skills to Help
You Deal with Anxiety,
Worry, and Sadness

978-1684039197 / US $22.95

JUST AS YOU ARE

A Teen's Guide to
Self-Acceptance and Lasting
Self-Esteem

978-1626255906 / US $17.95

🌱 new**harbinger**publications

1-800-748-6273 / newharbinger.com

(VISA, MC, AMEX / prices subject to change without notice)   Follow Us 🄾🄾🄾🄾🄾🄾🄾🄾🄾

Don't miss out on new books from New Harbinger.
Subscribe to our email list at **newharbinger.com/subscribe** 🖱

Did you know there are **free tools** you can download for this book?

Free tools are things like **worksheets**, **guided meditation exercises**, and **more** that will help you get the most out of your book.

You can download free tools for this book— whether you bought or borrowed it, in any format, from any source—from the New Harbinger website. All you need is a NewHarbinger.com account. Just use the URL provided in this book to view the free tools that are available for it. Then, click on the "download" button for the free tool you want, and follow the prompts that appear to log in to your NewHarbinger.com account and download the material.

You can also save the free tools for this book to your **Free Tools Library** so you can access them again anytime, just by logging in to your account! Just look for this button on the book's free tools page.

+ Save this to my free tools library

If you need help accessing or downloading free tools, visit **newharbinger.com/faq** or contact us at **customerservice@newharbinger.com**.